MW01484445

Copyright (c) 2016 Michael Hurd
Formerly known under the title of "The Visitor's Log"
(c) 1999 Michael Hurd
Cover Art by: Emily Ostrum © 2012
ISBN: 978-1-387-05333-9

ISBN 978-1-387-05333-9

90000
9 781387 053339

While reading this book, you will discover many lies.

In their discovery, you will find that you have embarked upon a journey to finding the truth behind those lies.

Please continue...

You are sleeping...quietly listening,
stay.
Do not awaken...just yet.
There is only gentleness...in all that is.

All is well, ...gentle sleeper.

Your eyes are closed,
You're only listening, for now.
find Patience.

Trust, in that we will not leave you........
For we have never been away.......

You may awaken now, gentle friend,
though you will yet, be asleep.

Table of Contents   <u>Page</u>

Article One – This Book

Chapter 1

This is what you have chosen; to be with us; now, and in this place.

You now hold the means within the palm of your hand; soft, receptive fingers cradling, as an anchoring thumb keeps our image in steady balance.

You hold to us, as we to you; in these quiet moments of reflection and limitless imagining. We are companions, and it has always been this way; though many times you had forgotten, and ran, to the slightest distraction. Still, and with great Love, we wait patiently for your return.

And just who, or what are we, exactly?

Has it really been so long, fitful sleeper, that you've lost the ability to recognize us? Have you so easily forgotten who we are to you, that it has now become necessary for us to approach you in this way? Is your memory so lost to this little world, that you cannot remember the *Home* that awaits your return? Don't let it worry you; it's only a small matter, and will easily be corrected.

**All is truly valued in one's remembering,
not in their forgetfulness.**

For now, simply and with your eyes; see us in a way that could never cause to threaten, or harm you. We are here for you now, just as you see us; as these printed words, even and oddly numbered pages, a binding, ...yes, this book!

Chapter 2

Maybe this little reunion of ours, isn't quite as exciting as you had imagined. When the thought of "contact" comes into your mind, it doesn't usually conjure up images of you, sitting and reading from a stack of printed-paper. We see so many of you, waiting around for something so absolutely amazing to happen, when closer to the truth, these early stages of contact are a much simpler kind of experience. They need to be, and it's not for our sake, but for yours... all of you.

Of course, the exciting bits *will* come, but it's important that you move through these simpler experiences first, to make sure that you can handle the really big ones when they do come. Does this make good sense to you? Shouldn't we learn to play scales before symphonies?

The early stages of many processes can sometimes seem slow and uninteresting; when you'd rather skip ahead to your 'heart's desire.' It is because that's where you believe your happiness lies.

Everyone wants to feel happiness.

We understand your feelings. But, the limits of your world force you to accept the fact that everything takes time. There are no real 'short-cuts' to success. It's possible that you can even remember a time when you experienced this fact for yourself. At that moment in your life, you knew that your goal couldn't have been accomplished in any other way, not if it was to last. Each step was needed for the final outcome. In the end, the whole process seemed to make perfect sense to you, even though there were some difficult times along the way.

Now, while you can accept all of this as being true, for some reason your human nature still continues to hope for an easier way of reaching your goals. There's no need to feel bad, because this kind of hope isn't about avoiding the work needed for success; it's about your wonderful ability to clearly imagine your ultimate goal, as if it were actually there with you in that moment. You're actually able to see the future while living in the present.

Unfortunately, it's only a possible future for you. You're still faced with the challenge of making it actually happen. You can see your goal; it seems real for you; but you're separated from it by a little thing called time. This bit of trouble doesn't seem to keep many humans from achieving their goals in life, however. It is a wonderful strength, and one that you possess. In the face of all of life's difficulties, you still manage to discover hope.

Hope connects you with patience.

Contacting you in this way is not so much a one-time event, as an ongoing process. You should also know that this is not the first step in that process. You've been connected with it for some time now; you just weren't aware of it. Until today, much of what was happening didn't really get your attention. It was happening, but you didn't notice. Now you have noticed, and your eyes are beginning to open.

Knowing your desires, we had thought to offer a more exciting way of introducing ourselves. You enjoy the meaningful experiences. After all, they leave you with the memories of a remarkable lifetime. We considered an experience similar to that of "love at first sight", but as you probably know, that kind of experience doesn't always last. Memories and feelings often begin to change and fade-away with time. Even the special memories will change, as you grow personally. This is quite natural and it happens because you're looking at these memories in new ways.

When something appears for us as a process it's always with us, always fresh in our mind. That's because it's happening right now. No matter where we are or what we're doing, we can always turn our thoughts to it, and it will be there for us. We can depend on it. Another thing we can say about any process in your world is that they all have a beginning and an end. We've already mentioned to you that contact is already taking place; you can rely on this. And you shouldn't worry that the process of contact will go on forever. It will end, once it has reached its limit. Your world has its limits and this is a good thing. It's another thing you can depend on. Are you beginning to feel how gentle and gradual the process is, now? We want contact to be real for you; we want you to feel that it's dependable; and we want it to last. The contact process is important to us and we hope that it will be just as important for you.

**Let us consider 'contact' as
the process of getting to know one another.**

Even though we've just told you that the process would be a simple one, that doesn't always mean it will be easy. The so-called rules of getting to know each other will be simple enough, but actually carrying them through will call for some minor adjustments on both our parts. There's no need for you to worry, we have plenty of time, and through most of it you probably won't even notice the changes are taking place. The process is that gradual, that simple, and what's even better, you can control the pace just as easily as opening and closing this book.

And why did we choose to come to you in this way? Well, if you must know, it was *you* who made the choice. If we remember correctly, we didn't exactly jump into your hand, and we didn't pay for ourselves—now did we? It was you! You had your choice from endless possibilities and you chose this one. You chose it because it was the right one for you. This isn't the only way we're approaching your kind. As you know, the world is a big place and with many different kinds of personalities, so we've had to come-up with all sorts of ways to catch everyone's attention. All of these different ways also have to be just as easy for the others, as this was for you. This way is your way, and though it may be pretty good for someone else, it may not be what's best for them. When their chosen time and place for contact arrives, they will recognize it.

You see, absolutely everyone is part of the overall plan. If anyone is left out, the process of contact won't work. It has to be balanced, and it has to be "all or nothing." We realize this sounds a little severe for you right now, so we will just leave it for the moment, and come back to it later. When we do, you'll understand it in a new way and it won't seem like such a big deal. This is just one of those "simple" steps we talked about earlier; the one's that help you get ready for the really big events. You might want to take a short break from your reading now.

Chapter 3

While reading this book, you may notice that some of the information seems a little odd, that it shows up in funny ways, and with little explanation. For instance, right now we're going to tell you that this book is alive. That's right, it's *Alive!*

Is this really so difficult to believe? Humans have grown to believe in so many outrageous things, would it be so strange to add this one to the list? Maybe this is just a little strange for you. After all, here you are, reading a book. It doesn't really look like it's alive, it doesn't feel alive, but at the same time, it's trying to get your attention through the sharing of a little friendly conversation. Isn't reading nothing more than a kind of private conversation between a book and its reader? We'll admit, and it's probably obvious to you by now, we will be getting a little more personal with you than many of the other books you've been reading lately. Our own style of speaking with you will eventually move beyond the simple exercise of "reading", to a more advanced level; one of actually communicating with you.

Have you noticed that, while you're reading these words with your eyes, you're also 'listening' to them within your mind? As your eyes sweep across line after line, don't you also "hear" the words speaking to you, in a kind of silent 'voice'? This will be our voice to you, and we offer it as a simple demonstration; that the written word may 'speak', and that a book may 'live' beyond its pages; even so far as to serve as constant companion. All books are more than just books; in their own way, they are very much alive!

We'll admit that the 'voice' you're now hearing does seem to bear an amazing resemblance to the voice you use for things like cursing, laughing, whispering, and storytelling. As well, this 'voice' will sound a lot like the one you hear in your head, whenever you're doing any sort of thinking, reading or muttering under your breath. So, just whose voice is it, anyway? Is it yours, or is it ours? The answer is both. The voice you're now experiencing is pretty much yours, but we're going to be borrowing it for a little while. We knew you wouldn't mind.

In order to make this phase of the contact process as comfortable as possible, we felt that using your own voice would probably be the best way of reaching you. If we had chosen to use any other style of voice, while it might have been a little more entertaining, eventually it would have led to some problems with the strength of our connection. Instead of seeing us as familiar, we would have appeared strange, maybe even "alien." If there's one thing you can be sure of, we're not strangers to one another. The ability to imitate your voice comes as part of a specially designed plan for entering into your world. Isn't there a saying on your planet that goes something like "there's nothing so sweet as the sound of one's own voice?" Wouldn't you agree that using this voice; *your* voice, is the better way?

Now, we're going to be using this charming little voice of yours in a couple of different ways. The first one should be fairly obvious, as you follow along with the text of this message. The second way will be a little sneakier. You see, we had to find some way of keeping you 'in touch' during those times when you weren't reading from this book. It's clear, that if you decided, right now, to close its covers, this action would instantly stop our little conversation from continuing. And having done so, we would lose your attention, or, in other words, our connection with you. We only appear for you during those times when you choose to give us your complete attention. Reading is a great way to get this attention, because while reading you tend to 'tune-out' the rest of the world around you. This second way of using your voice is for those times when you're not 'tuned-in.'

If you were to close this book for a few moments, you would start to see what it is we're talking about. As you turn away from these pages, the voice doesn't stop. Sure, the conversation stops, but the voice goes into a 'playback' mode; sending certain key words like "waffles" bouncing around in your head for hours, and even days after you've read them. These words will carry-on, as a little echo within your mind. They will live on and on, skipping to the very beginnings of your human brain, and then back again. The human brain loves to keep busy, and when there's no new information to process, it quickly revisits previous images and data for you. This is part of its job.

As a small demonstration of this occasionally annoying, but useful side-effect, we would like to invite you to gently, close your eyes for one or two moments of peace. Try, if you will, to think of something else; something different from what we have just been talking about. Notice, just how long you're able to do this, without returning, once again, to the subject of our discussion.

The choice to perform this short exercise is completely your own.

Chapter 4

Returning to our discussion, we now find ourselves in the position of challenging one of your closely guarded human beliefs, the one that considers all of the objects within your world as essentially 'dead.' We don't move around, or grow, or eat so we must be dead, right? Well that's what you've been led to believe, isn't it? You weren't actually told to think anything different, so why should you believe that we're alive just because we say so? With all your abilities for imagining all kinds of wild and wonderful things, wouldn't it be just as easy for you to believe that this little book in your hand was alive? If it's possible to imagine one, is it so hard to imagine the other? "But," you say, "I can't prove that it's alive. I have no real way of showing to anyone that it's alive." And, just who is it you need to prove this to, anyway? There is no one but yourself who needs convincing. When all is said and done, you only need to prove it to yourself.

With all of your knowledge of science and of how things appear in your world, it's easy to accept that the paper book and its pages were made from some sort of tree. Now, even though you might not be able to physically see the actual tree from which the book was made, it's still possible to assume that this tree was once, very much alive. Try to imagine that great, silent companion of the forest, whose strong limbs once extended sweet shelter to one such as yourself. It doesn't matter which tree, or what kind of tree it was, what we're concerned with here, is whether or not you believe the tree actually lived. We sense no immediate disagreement from you, so we'll continue.

This tree once held the essence, or energy, which brought it to live, and helped it to grow. We will call this essence *Life*. There's no need for us to go into much detail regarding this concept, so we won't. Let's just say that *Life* is simply, that built-in capability; responsible for the seeming growth and evolutionary change of all life forms. You can't actually see it right now, but you can see what it does; you can see its effects. As you've watched the physical changing and growing of those around you, the 'spark' responsible for those changes came from their *Life*. This impulse, or push started as a hidden possibility within them, and later transformed them in such a way, that it resulted in the experience of movement, or change. And when you saw these changes happening, it told you that this thing or person was alive. It lived because it grew, changed and moved for you.

Now, assuming that the tree was once alive, does it still live? Does our old friend still exist, even after having been chopped apart and made into a book? If you were to ask us this question we would say that, from where we see things, the tree is definitely still alive. But, since we've asked you, it would seem the answer you're about to give us, is the opposite. In many ways, you believe the tree has been destroyed and is now dead. We'll admit the tree appears to be gone, but is it actually dead?

"All *Life* shall persist."

The answer to this question is to be found within this simple statement. This is one of the Keys to your existence; just one of the answers you are currently seeking.

Even though you aren't able to physically see it right now, the Life of something or someone is always here. No matter what shape or form it may, or may not take; it's always around you. We don't see something as dead, just because it no longer appears to us, as it once was. What we see is that a change has taken place, and that things now look different from before that change. You might take a minute to remember those exciting days in Science class, when your teacher tried to tell you all about Energy. They taught you that all of the Energy in the Universe lives-on in one way or another. It never really goes away, it just changes the way it behaves, or how it looks. Whether it was called Potential Energy, Kinetic Energy, or Nuclear Energy, these were all just some way of describing that stuff called Energy. In this discussion we've called it *Life*, but in truth, they're all the same thing.

Now, as our tree has stopped looking like a tree, and started looking like a book, we can safely assume that it has simply changed its appearance for a while. In truth, the tree does still exist, but in disguise. This complex process of transformation is achieved in many different ways; both known and unknown to you, at this time. The part you know about is the cutting and the processing; but there is another, very important part of the process, going on "behind the scenes." We won't be looking at this business of the unknown just yet, but we do realize that it's important to you.

We're very happy to see that a large part of your mind is now busy visualizing the process we've been describing. It's obvious that you understand the physical part of this process, very well. And, while those 'unknowns' sit just out of reach, you're very close to seeing them. You have the ability to bridge the gap in your mind, which separates you from the unknown. And, being able to use this natural ability will prove to be very important, if we are to proceed with any degree of success.

Chapter 5

Let's take a little break from the discussion to think about something.

What if the tree, you're now 'seeing' in your mind, were the actual tree from which this book was made? The book you're now holding, in essence, carries a memory with it; a record of its existence; of its lifetime. And as you might have guessed, it's a hidden or invisible memory. From seed to sapling, to a full-grown tree and now, this book; all of the stages in the tree's lifetime, have been carefully recorded. As you hold this book in your hands, you possess more than just a physical connection with the tree; you also hold the key to its hidden life. Let's show you what we mean. For the next couple of minutes, we would like you to close this book and picture in your mind which part of the tree you might actually be holding. Is it a piece of a branch, or part of the trunk? Is there any bark in it? Hold on to this picture, and 'see' it clearly, as you build a connection between the tree, the book and yourself.

This simple exercise is meant to bring you to an awareness, or way of seeing things, that goes beyond using your human eyes. This kind of 'seeing' with the hands and mind is well known in your world; though for many of you, putting the information to use is still just a lot of "hocus pocus." It's an entertaining trick, but why would anyone actually want to take it seriously, right?

Psychometry, as it is commonly known, is basically an exercise in information gathering. The type of information that one "picks-up" can be related to all sorts of things: Where does the object come from? How old is it? What is it feeling? Literally, anything you touch can be a source of information for you, if you're open to receiving it. How do you feel about Psychometry? Is it real for you, or were you just imagining things? Do you feel that having this kind of information is dangerous?

We can understand that it isn't always easy to completely accept the reality of those abilities, which are now only beginning to awaken in you. We know that you're worried about what others might think and say, and of how they will treat you, because of them. The purpose of these new abilities is still so unknown, and you will all feel a lot of doubt and fear until you get used to having them around.

Your feelings are completely natural.

The purpose of these feelings is to help regulate how fast these new talents awaken within you. They're here to make the process more gradual, so that you won't be overwhelmed when they come to you in full force. Please don't think of your feelings as being, 'bad', they can often be very helpful.

When you 'saw' those pictures of the tree in your mind, you were receiving a message. In its own way, the tree was trying to tell you that it was still alive. If it had actually been dead, you would have seen nothing, for how could something that was dead communicate with you? Please believe us when we say that, what you 'saw' was more than just your imagination.

Chapter 6

Now, back to the discussion...

For whatever reasons, this tree of ours has chosen a new lifestyle. Yes, that's right, the tree actually played a big part in this decision. After all, why wouldn't it? If something this important concerned you, wouldn't you want to be involved? We understand that the thought of what we're saying can be very upsetting to many of you, but it must be said. In time, all of this will become clearer, and things will make more sense. This is an important time of preparation for all of you. We don't expect you to completely accept all that we're saying, only to think about it.

This decision by the tree is completely acceptable to us. We're in no position to say whether a decision is 'right', or 'wrong', 'bad', or 'good.' You, however, seem to be in a position to pass judgment on these things. We can see that these acts of destruction are offensive to many of you, and even though you might have chosen to do so, we will not judge them. Please don't be too disappointed in us. We know you expected us to be a little more supportive in these matters; but we have to be honest with you. We have to respect the conditions of Free will that exist for you and the others. This complete freedom to choose exists not just for humans, but for all of existence on your planet. Even our tree has the right to choose how it will live, or change.

Freewill is not exclusive.

Soon, you'll notice that the 'style' of writing in this book will have changed. When it does, it'll seem more like our conversation is on a "person to person" level. It won't seem so cold and unfeeling. When this happens, it's possible that the personality speaking with you, will want to offer their opinions on many subjects. You might agree with them, or not. The choice is yours. Either way, these personalities are a necessary part of the discussion. You will gradually come to see their purpose. If it makes you feel any better, we'll spare you from their influence when we can.

Now, as our dear tree has given up a part of its previous life to make this page, it has en-livened it for us. It has given some of its life to, and for this book. To give life doesn't mean to choose death, nor does it involve any sacrifice. It's more about sharing what one has, or what one is. As we've said, there is freedom to choose within your world, however, Cosmic Suicide is not on the list of available choices. If it were, it would go against the primary rule of existence; "All Life shall persist". One may not agree to end its primary existence. No one can change what they are, in truth. There are no exceptions to this rule.

In a dramatic performance of chop and slash, the tree has appeared to meet a gruesome death; it's branches and bark scattered all over the forest floor, and all for the production of a few books and maybe some lumber.

One may not cease to exist,
however,
One may *pretend* to do so.

Maybe this isn't the kind of pretending you're used to, but it's still considered to be just that.

What's happened, basically, is the tree has chosen to present the illusion of its destruction. There was no real loss of life. This production was arranged to demonstrate an aspect of Change. Unfortunately, anyone witnessing this performance would've thought that they were seeing something else.

How something 'appears' to you and what that something really 'is', are very different with respect to their intentions. As well, the way that something 'appears' for one person will often look very different to someone else. They're both looking at the same thing, but seeing it in different ways. Neither person is completely right about what they think they're seeing, but both have done their best, in trying to figure it out. All of this is perfectly understandable to you, having experienced these types of situations in your own life. These misunderstandings exist because of the unique ways in which all of you experience your world. More importantly, they also result from a severe lack of information, or the truth. When you don't have all the facts about what's going-on, it's hard to know what's really happening. It's easy to make a mistake. We're here to help you find that missing information.

There's no need for you to worry. Our friend the tree is very much alive and well, and for the time being, in your protective care. She wouldn't have wanted it any other way. As you hold this book, feel her life moving into your hands; running up, and then down your arms. She's sharing with you. She's sharing *us* with you. This is how we feel. There and here, is *Life*.

Chapter 7

If you'll just take a minute to remember what we were discussing in Chapter Five, we can begin to show you another side of Psychometry; one which reveals it as a tool for remembering.

When a person uses this ability, the kind of information they can receive is definitely not the sort you will find using your everyday, physical senses. It will show you a much deeper world; one that takes you closer to the real nature of the object. At this advanced level, you will actually begin to experience the object, in some way. You won't just be seeing it, or touching it; you will actually begin to feel some of its feelings, and even take part in some of its memories.

The process follows several important rules; the most important one is, of course, being given permission to do so. You've got to have permission from the object before you can start gathering information from it. After all, it's only polite. It's not possible to just read any old stone whenever you feel like it, expecting the information to just start flowing to you. No matter how odd this might seem, something has to be offered to you, before you can receive it. Your ability to gather information will depend very much upon the source of that information. If the stone prefers not to share itself with you, then the process will never begin. Thankfully, this rarely happens, as *Life*, and stones, generally enjoy sharing with others.

The process of sharing information or memories is more like an agreement between the object and the reader. Both must play their part. The reader simply opens by asking the stone to begin remembering. If this is acceptable to the stone, it will then choose certain memories that will help to answer the reader's questions. Ideally, the activity should have some useful purpose. The information should be *helpful*, in some way.

As you begin practicing with different objects, you will find that a slight 'opening' starts to form within your mind, allowing little bits of simple information to pass through. It's a lot like the opening you're experiencing right now, with us. In our case, you're seeing the information coming to you as these words, and hearing it as a silent voice. With some honest practice, your viewpoint will begin to change. You will begin to sense, to feel, and experience the information in a much deeper and personal way. Eventually, our style of communicating will seem quite shallow in comparison to your newfound talent. That's not to say that our way is any less important. In the process of evolution, all experiences are important, for they provide us with the necessary "stepping stones" to a better way of living.

As we've already said, this is a sharing process. The information is not so much given to you, as it is shared with you. Although it is held out to you, the information will always remain connected with its source. You cannot take it away from the stone. If this is the case, then how do you actually receive the information? Is it possible to receive something that never leaves the one who offers it? Yes, it is possible. The act of sharing is actually a blending of your awareness with that of another. Try and imagine it, if you will. To a certain extent, there is a joining or focusing that takes place between the two of you. You blend with one another. (You're doing very well with picturing it in your mind.) The blending doesn't have to be complete, and it rarely ever is. It usually only goes as far as it needs to, in serving the purposes of the reading. The process is specific and selective and works very well. As it's taking place, the two of you become essentially the same being, while experiencing the memory. You are both remembering. Yes, the reader is also remembering. Although these aren't actually their memories, the reader may occasionally begin to feel as though they are.

This experience is perfectly acceptable, and even encouraged. Taking the time to use your ability in Psychometry will be very helpful to you as you enjoy remembering for and with, many objects. As a final note, the amount of memory experienced during these times depends, to a large extent, upon the degree of desire present within the reader. The more you want the information, the more information you'll get. That is all.

Chapter 8

What is memory? Do you feel that you've come to a point in this lifetime when, and where you can say that you are honestly prepared to appreciate the true nature and function of your memory? Are you ready to experience the totality of your existence within each and every passing moment? With complete and total recollection there is such intensity of experience, such utter rapture.

Possession of such knowledge and awareness of being would be sufficient to presently obliterate the person you have come to know as your person. Are you prepared to undergo such an incredible transformation?

Well, perhaps not just yet (And maybe we are getting just a little dramatic.)

Funny enough, the time for this transformation is actually coming, and we're here to make sure you're ready. A little groundwork is always helpful, especially concerning *The Revealing.*

In the previous chapter, we showed you an experience that is very close to that of actual memory, or remembering. It was a training experience for you. Real memory, all memories, exists as shared information, or common knowledge. They live as the memory of *The One.* Our very own collective memory exists along with yours and with countless others as well. It's all-together the same thing.

If this is true, then why don't you experience it this way? If what we're saying is true; and all memories are common knowledge, then you should now be experiencing complete access to all kinds of information. All that ever was and is, within and without all of existence, should be yours for the taking. But, this doesn't seem to be the case now does it? So, why is it, this wealth of knowledge and information are being kept from you? Who is doing this to you? Truthfully, this memory isn't being kept from you; it has always been available, anytime you needed it. It is you who is keeping it from you. Hidden within you, is an understanding of the true nature of this memory. On this level, you understand that all knowledge brings with it a great responsibility. Maybe you don't want this responsibility right now. Maybe you're afraid that it might be too much for you to handle. How do you feel about responsibility?

Although you may not notice it, when you use your memory you come-up against all kinds of invisible, carefully placed areas where you believe you can't go. Let's think of remembering as being like the process of walking down a hallway with many doors. You're looking for something and you begin trying the door handles, to see if any of the doors will let you in. As you do this, you find that some of them are locked, and some are open to you. This is normal. But, because you found that some of the doors were locked the first time, you never tried them again. You thought they'd always be locked for you. After a while, you started to ignore these doors completely and eventually even forgot they existed. You only went to those areas where you knew the doors would be open to you. And you went to these doors again and again. Of all the possible doors in your memory that were there for you, you chose a certain section of them and have kept to that area for most of your lifetime. Imagine everything you've ever known, or thought about in your lifetime. Think of all the places and the people and the experiences you've known. Now, imagine that all of this is just a little area within your mind. Now imagine all that lies still waiting for you!

When you were young, you were very curious. So, one day you began to search through the halls of your mind, looking for things and ideas to play with. You started trying all of those little doors and found that some of them were open, some were locked, and some had handles that you couldn't quite reach. This was a lot of fun for you. But, then one day you thought that all of this exploring was a lot of work, and so you thought about making maps for yourself. These mental maps were specially designed so that you could get to the open doors much easier. Using them, you could find all of your favorite places much, much faster. When you drew the maps you only put in the doors you knew, why bother with the other ones, right? There were so many doors to draw into your maps, they couldn't possibly all fit. So you left many out. These early maps are the very same ones you're using today.

Even as you move through your world from day to day, don't you find that you follow the same old routes? How often do you honestly take a different road to get to where you're going? This is what we're talking about. You have a lot of different reasons for not going into certain areas in your mind, as well as within the outside world; and we've heard them all, so there's no need trying to explain yourself. To us, the reasons don't really matter, what's important is that you admit to yourself that there are lots of new places, within your mind, that might be worth seeing. These forgotten "doors" are worth a second try. After all this time, they're still waiting for you, and you might just find that some of them are now ready for you to open. The experiences of this lifetime have prepared you for what's on the other side of those doors. We know it's a big job having to go back and find them, but there's plenty of time. We won't rush you; we just want you to think about them for now.

If you feel ready to begin searching, we'll give you a little help. In order to successfully uncover these long-forgotten areas, you will need to remember a time when you were very young. This was when you made those early maps, and so using these memories will help you to see the doors you missed. You might want to look for one of your old toys, or a photograph of yourself, at that age. If these aren't around, a short walk through your old neighborhood, or your old home can really help. Touch these objects and places with your hands. Gently close your eyes, and remember.

Chapter 9

We've noticed there are a few problems in the way you've been using your memory. This chapter isn't really related to those problems, though you might start to think it is.

For one reason or another, it seems your memory doesn't always work so well. Sometimes you forget. No matter how you try, the information just won't come to mind. Of course, the first idea that comes to you is that it's a memory problem. It's not. There is nothing wrong with your memory. In fact, you carry a perfect record of absolutely everything that has happened in this lifetime, right down to the tiniest, sweetest, tastiest cookie crumb.

Forgetting things is more related to how a person pays attention. (Are you still thinking about that cookie?) When you start to concentrate on the things and people in your world, the act of concentrating takes place in an area of the mind called the *Attention Space*. In any given moment, it is within this little section that you will cram all of what's happening to you on the outside, plus all of what you're thinking about on the inside. It's a very crowded space, but it doesn't need to be. When you find it difficult to remember something, you've probably filled your *Attention Space* to its limit. There isn't room for anything else. In order to bring something else into this space, like a memory for instance, you will have to find some way to make room for it.

Let's think of your *Attention Space* as a desk, in the middle of a busy office. It's a small space, but it's all yours. Things are very hectic for you here; the telephone is ringing, there are heaps of files on your desk, lots of little bits of paper containing messages, ideas and reminders. There's garbage from a half-eaten lunch of some sort and, of course, someone is tapping you on the shoulder, trying to get you to answer his, or her questions.

Is it possible to fit anything else into this picture? It's possible, but first, something has got to go. You're going to have to do a little re-organizing and of course, this is going to take some time. That's all perfectly well, but until that time has passed, you won't be able to remember what it is you think, you forgot. Have you ever noticed that after you've had the chance to relax a little, your mind gradually begins to clear and then *pop*, the very thing you were trying to remember has now, suddenly dropped into your mind, and come to your full attention?

Chapter 10

How does a person remember? What's the best way for you to find all of the many hidden treasures, stored within memory? First of all, you need to stop thinking about it. You might be surprised to learn that thinking isn't always the best way of doing things. In the case of remembering, it uses too much energy, and the results can be unreliable. A better way of remembering involves 'feeling' for the information. We would like you to try locating memories by using certain feelings, or emotions.

When you remember people and events from your past, do you ever find that certain feelings seem to come along with those memories? Do these personal feelings sometimes make you imagine that you're in another place and time? When the memory is really clear, the feelings will be almost identical to the ones you originally felt. It's an amazing experience, but isn't this also one of the reasons why we like to remember? Aren't we trying to recapture a feeling of happier moments? Simply picturing something with your mind can be dull and flat, but to really feel it, now that's enjoyable. Human feelings of pleasure and pain can be so moving. They can take us away from day-to-day routines, and add a richness that makes your lifetime seem worthwhile. These feelings are part of the reason you're here.

One day soon, we're going to ask you to remember something. When we do, we will ask you to feel for the memory, rather than think. We're warning you now, because we want you to be ready. We don't want it to be a surprise. When we ask, we will want you to re-experience an important time and place. We will want you to "be" there, and really feel that you're there, but also to know that you're only remembering. In *Reality*, you're safe and sound, no matter what you might be remembering at that time. If this sounds a bit confusing, you don't need to worry. When the time comes, the activity won't be difficult for you. You'll be completely ready for it.

When you try to think your way to a memory, you run the risk of finding a memory that may not actually be real. This is what we mean when we say that 'thinking' for memories can be unreliable. These memories will be close to the real ones, but they won't actually be true. You see, when someone tries to remember by 'thinking', they start *building* a memory. The human mind is a wonderful tool for building and constructing. When it finds bits and pieces of a real memory, it quickly tries to fill-in the missing gaps because it's in a hurry. What the mind needs is patience. The so called, 'missing' pieces of memory aren't actually missing; they just haven't arrived yet. If your mind would be willing to wait a little longer, you'll quickly see the difference between fiction and the truth.

The truth is always worth waiting for.

Your memory is an old friend. It understands you and cares for you, in a way that few people can. It knows the deepest and most personal parts of you; all your secrets and all of your dreams. It knows you so well, in fact, that it can sense when life's little mysteries are getting you down. When something goes wrong, your memory knows just what you need, to get back on track. And, what's more, you never need to ask for its help. Isn't that what good friends are for? Your memory knows you, and it knows how to help you. Your memories aren't simply there for you to flip through, like some old photo album. Memories have an important place in your life; they're your personal source of wisdom. Within your memory, you will find all of the answers to the problems of your everyday life.

Let's think about your life for a moment. No matter how long you've been living, you've managed to scrape together a lot of personal experience. Hidden within all of this experience, are the many lessons you learned about getting along in the world. Some of these lessons were learned from others, and some of them you had to learn the "hard way." Either way, these lessons can still be helpful. It doesn't matter if it's been a long time since you've used some of them; they're still ready to be pulled off the shelf and put to use. If you're having problems with this, it may be because some of the information isn't easy for you to recognize. In the case of some memories, it's been so long since you've looked at them that you may not remember what they look like. This can lead to some confusion when they decide to show up. The memory will look strange to you and you'll just 'shrug' it off. When this happens, your memory doesn't know how to get the information to you. Without easy access to this information, the problems in your life take longer to solve. This can lead to frustration. Your memory gets frustrated with you and you get frustrated with this lifetime. Without proper access to your personal log of wisdom, you're not able to "live life to the fullest." You're not getting "the most out of life."

It's a funny thing, but many of you still believe that one day you'll hear a great and powerful voice from above, telling you exactly what you need to do next. Sadly, and no matter what anyone tells you, that's not how things work in your world. We agree, it would be much easier if it did work that way, but we're in no position to change any of the rules. Thankfully, all the information you need is already in your possession. The 'great and powerful voice' you're needing to hear actually sounds a lot more like the one you're hearing right now.

The voice you're needing to hear, is your own.

The wisdom you seek will always come to you as a memory of something that happened in your life. It comes to you this way, so that you'll recognize it. It's personalized. Your memory is saying, "Remember when this happened? Well, you can use what you learned back then, for the situation you're facing now." On the outside, it might seem as if they're two totally different problems, but when you take a closer look, you'll see that the answers to both of them are the same. The two problems are directly related. In *Reality*, they're the same problem; they're just wearing different disguises. A person really doesn't need to know a whole lot about the world, in order to survive, or be successful. In fact, you've pretty well learned all of the important lessons before the age of about seven years. These simple and effective solutions can be used over, and over again.

Your memory looks a lot like a big warehouse. It's filled with different kinds of pictures, objects, animals, colors and people. Some of these you'll recognize and some will look very strange to you. All of it is your memory. For the sake of keeping everything organized, your memory takes whole events from your life, and files each of them as a single object. Each object is totally unique. This way your memories won't get mixed up with one another. As you might imagine, this can lead to quite a collection of objects.

It would be almost impossible for anyone to be able to keep track of all the different memory objects, within their personal warehouse. Thankfully, you don't have to. Your memory automatically does the work for you. It knows where everything is and what it's for. All you need to do is trust that it will do its job. When we speak of trusting your memory, we mean *allowing* it to do its job. Don't try to interfere, or help it in any way. Your memory knows what it's doing, even if it doesn't look that way.

When searching for something in your memory, all you need to do is ask for the information and wait. This kind of waiting will not be boring for you. Your memory will start sending you images that will lead you to the information you want or need. It will take you on a trip through your warehouse of memories, presenting you with all kinds of mental images. Hold onto each image for a moment or two, and see what happens. As you hold onto them or pay attention to them, they will begin opening for you. Each image is a package that contains the memory of an experience. When it opens, you will remember something, and this will either give you the information you want, or it will give you part of the information, and you will then need to open the next object, to receive another part of the information. The number of objects you'll need to open will depend on how complicated your question is. If this sounds simple, it's because it *is* simple. It was meant to be that way. If you have any problems in using these steps at first, you'll probably find that they show up in the step where you're trying to grab hold of the mental images. The images will seem to come very quickly at first. Being part of your mind, your memory works very efficiently. Don't worry if you happen to miss any of the images; they will come back around again for you. Like any new task, it will get much easier with just a little practice.

Some of the images you will be seeing might not seem related to your questions; they might even shock you, from time to time. Try not to reject them. They can help. Your mental filing system might seem a little unusual, but it *does* work. With practice, you will move into some advanced memory work, and this is where things will start to get really interesting.

While your human mind is working, it does everything it can to make connections. It tries to relate your thoughts, memories, experiences and ideas together in special ways. It never leaves anything to stand on its own. Connecting one thing with another makes them both easier to find. If you want, you can imagine that there are little strings tied to everything in your brain. Nothing ever gets lost, and one thing always leads to another.

Grabbing-on to one idea tugs a little on those connecting strings, bringing other ideas along for you to see. This starts a "chain reaction" as ideas and memories start to shape an answer to your question. This process is called *Solution Building*, and it gives you some different ways of looking at a problem. To make the best choices, you'll first need to look at a problem in a few different ways. Looking at a problem from only one angle won't give you the whole picture. When you're too close to the problem, mistakes can happen. Imagining other possibilities allows you to gently step away from your problem so you can see it more clearly and find a better answer. Remember.

Chapter 11

We've told you, that we're here for you in the form of this book. This much is clear. But, the time has come for us to tell you a little more. Soon, that original explanation won't be enough for you. You're very curious, and we can see that you'll need more information if we're going to keep your attention for much longer.

Closer to the truth, we're a *Gathering*. We're not so much separate "beings", as a collection or group. Our life is a lot like yours. As the name implies, we are many, joined together as one. Being a group, this makes us One. The voice you've been listening to while reading this book is supported by all our individual voices. Can you imagine what it would be like if everyone in your world were to start talking together at the same time? If they were all saying the same thing, it would be a powerful voice, but since everyone would probably want to say something different, or in a different language, the voices would be hard to understand.

We weren't always this way. Once, we thought we were very separate from one another. Then came the experiment known as *The Great Unification*. Many said it couldn't be done, and still more said that it shouldn't, but there were enough of us who decided that it *had* to be done. And, so it was. You can imagine how afraid we were, thinking that when it *did* happen, we would lose all sense of who we were, as individuals. We thought we would forget our friends, and family, and all of the many wonderful experiences we all shared. We thought individually, we would all be washed away. There were so many things of which we couldn't be sure. Everything was just a theory of some kind, a possibility, with no real proof that everything would turn out alright. As you can see, everything turned out just fine. Actually, our coming together has produced some benefits we hadn't planned on. When we gathered together, the result was much more than the possibilities of simply adding our separate selves together. In other words, as The Gathering, we are now "more than the sum of our parts."

There is a great leap forward that takes place when separate individuals come together. If you were to think of the process of human evolution as slowly climbing a ladder, then our act of joining together was like suddenly skipping a few steps upward, on that ladder. There is a huge release of energy that takes place when something new and different comes from mixing together a few simple ingredients. It was this boost of energy that shot us up the evolutionary ladder, into this new way of living.

When we joined together, it did not take away our individuality. Surprisingly, it was the opposite. Since the unification, we now have a better understanding of what it means to be individuals. We're able to see ourselves in relation to everyone and everything else, and all at the same time. It's amazing to think how many times we used to assume that others were just like us. What a mistake. Now we have a much clearer idea of who and what we are, both as individuals and as The Gathering. This was a huge step for us, one that we could only have dreamed of achieving, before it actually happened. In fact, the change was so drastic, that there is no possible way for us to ever go back to the way we were. The choice is not reversible for us, and we don't ever regret making it.

At this moment, you might be wondering where we are, or if we've come from some other world. The best way we can answer this is to say that we are *Here*. *Here* isn't really a particular place. If someone were to ask you, "Where are you?" - the simplest way to answer them would be to say "Here". Close your eyes for a moment and try to feel what this means. No matter where you are, you're always "Here", aren't you? This is similar to how we feel. We don't have any sense of being near, or far. We're always, just *Here*. Now because of this, and because of the idea that you think you're in a certain place, you can't see us the way we really are. If we were in a certain place, then you *could* see us. This is because we would be outside of you, with some distance between us.

There isn't any distance between us.

Have you ever seen your face without a mirror? (Pictures don't count) This is what it's like. But, even though you can't see us, you can still have an experience of us. The way this happens is easy for you to understand, because we've already talked about it. It's called remembering. You are now remembering. You are remembering us.

Why have we come? In your lifetime, there were many times when you called out for help, strength, or an answer to your suffering. We are answering some of those calls for help, at this time. You might be wondering why we didn't come sooner, when you actually needed us. All we can say is that we *did* come, but you didn't recognize us. You wouldn't listen and you couldn't see. We've tried so many times to help you, but you weren't willing to accept us the way we were, so we had to find another way. Finally, it seems, this one is working for us.

We're here to re-mind you of your *Self*. We've come to take you *Home*. This doesn't mean that we're some alien race from a distant galaxy; coming to take you away from all your problems. We don't have a spaceship. We're sorry to disappoint you, if this was what you had in mind. If we thought it would help, we *would* use a spaceship. You see, going *Home* doesn't actually involve any traveling. If *Home* was an actual place, you'd be there. In truth, you're already *Home*. The problem is you don't know that your *Home*. You think you're somewhere else. You think you're this person, who's living on a nice little planet, just the right distance from a sun, that's whirling around through space and taking you with it. We're going to use an example to try and describe your situation for you. Please remember that it's just an example.

You've wandered into a "Funhouse", a highly complex "House of Mirrors". You've probably seen these at your local fairs, or on the television, so we don't need to tell you how they work. This one, however, is really big and really amazing, probably the best ever. It was designed so that it would be hard for anyone to tell the difference between what was real and what was just for show. This was serious entertainment. You paid the fare and just went looking for a little fun, but you found it to be better than anything you'd ever tried. It was so incredible that you decided to stay and enjoy yourself. While this was happening, however, you got more and more involved with what you were seeing. You weren't just browsing anymore.

In fact, you got so concerned with what was happening, that you started to forget that it was all just for fun. You started to actually believe in all the things you saw and heard, forgetting who you were and why you originally came to this place. You lost your grip on what the truth was; you believed in the voices of the Funhouse and stopped listening to your own.

It's hard for us to say how it all started, but while you were enjoying yourself, you became so addicted to this new way of living that you did something really unusual. You made a wish. You wished that the fun would never end. You hoped that you would never, ever go *Home*, and that you could stay and enjoy this world forever. It was at that very moment you started to believe that this "Funhouse" *was* your *Home*. And you've believed in it ever since.

You think this is your *Home*. It is not.

This place is called *Reality*. We're going to be talking a lot about *Reality*, mostly about how it works and how you can see your way clear to finding the way out. It's a very big place and the signs aren't always obvious, so you'll need a little help. For now, we'll just repeat why we're *Here*. We would like you to return *Home* with us. Everything you see around you, no matter how beautiful it might seem, is not your *Home*. It's your pretend home, your make-believe home. The choice is yours. You can stay and play with your friends as long as you like, but we've been getting the feeling, from all of your complaining, that you've lost interest in these games. We think you're ready now.

Everything you'll need for the first part of the trip is already in your possession. Any needed tools or abilities are already with you. You just need to remember them for what they are, and use them the way they were meant to be used. You've been using these same tools ever since you arrived, so they will be very familiar to you. Unfortunately, you've been using them to keep you here, instead of getting you *Home*. You've been using them backwards, in a way. We've come to help you switch them around, so they're pointing you in the direction of *Home*. If you feel that you're not quite ready to come with us, then we would like you to stop reading this book. Place the book safely on a shelf somewhere, until you feel you're ready. Until that time, anything you will read beyond this page won't be of any use to you, and it would only keep you from your fun. It has been a pleasure speaking with you.

We wish you well.

If you're reading these words, then you've chosen to return with us. Don't worry if you're only just reading them out of curiosity. All we need is just a little desire, just a hint that you're willing to listen to what we have to say to you, in order to make it work. Thank you for believing in us, and congratulations on your choice!

Since the moment you became lost to this world, we have not forgotten you. You have never been, nor will you ever be, without our undying love and understanding. We have always respected your choice, and we respect it still. No matter what you choose, we shall never leave you. We will always be with you.

Chapter 12

Let's think of this book as a symbol. This book stands for something. It embodies the whole reason we're here. It's a starting point. When you first opened this book, you performed a symbolic act. You opened your mind to what was waiting for you inside. At that moment, you let us in. It was a simple thing, but it meant a lot. These are the kinds of things that we will be asking you to do. Simple acts can be so important if we stop and realize what we're really doing, and why.

This starting point is the second most important part of your journey *Home*. The first is your *Reference Point*. From there, everything else will follow. The purpose of this beginning is to help guide you toward that *Reference Point*. After that, the trip *Home* becomes much easier. Once you reach that point, you won't need our help anymore. You'll be on your own, but you won't be alone. You'll have plenty of company.

Many of you believe that you're on "the path", that you're already headed for *Home*. You're on the path, that's true. But, from our point of view you seem to be standing still, or running on the spot. You're "spinning your wheels." Please don't think that we're trying to put you down, after all of the work you've done. We can see that you're doing your best. We need to tell you these things, so that you can honestly face your situation, and then move on. During this stage, we're going to help you retrace your steps.

Together, we're going to find the place and time, where you remember making the decision to stay here. We won't be taking these steps for you; we will be taking them *with* you. You'll have to take them for yourself. The steps you will be taking aren't physical ones, like when you're walking or running; they're decisions; they're choices. A person can do all the running around, and talking and reading they want, but until they actually make a choice, or *do* something about what they've learned, they haven't moved a bit. When this kind of false thinking happens, it's known as a *False Move*. It isn't a real move until the person carries it through.

It will seem like we're asking a lot from you in the beginning. We will need you to continue to trust what we're saying and we will also need you to really want this to be a success. This shouldn't be a problem for you; you've been ready and willing to make this journey for some time now. If you weren't ready, we couldn't have come this far together.

This beginning had two very important parts to it. The first, we said, was within your mind. But, before that happened, there was another, more important one. This one was within your heart, your emotional center.

To truly remember,
one must first open their heart.

This was when you decided to trust us. It took a lot of courage to face this part of the process, but we knew you'd be ready. We'd seen you face this kind of challenge before, and with great success.

Should you be acting this way? Do the others in your world tell you that you should trust so easily? We don't believe they do. "There's too much to worry about, you could get hurt. It's better to be careful until you're sure you can really trust, and even then, you might still get hurt. Being open and trusting can make you look weak in the eyes of other people. It's not the way you want to be. You want to be strong, in control, and sure of yourself and what you're doing, right?"

We'd like to warn you now, that when you actually listen to what we have to say and begin to make real changes, you will start to seem a little foolish to your friends and family. They might say things that will make you think twice about this new information. Try not to take them too seriously, they want to help you in their own way, but they don't really understand what's happening. To be open, or to see someone else being open, is pretty rare nowadays. No matter what might happen in the future and no matter how you'll appear to everyone else, you will be in complete control of your thoughts and actions.

Attention!

Here are a few simple guidelines, some notes to help make things easier for each of us. We won't go into much detail right now, because you'll see them again, later in the book. Don't think of them as rules. They're just a little something, to get you started. We're not asking you to believe in any of them. That's up to you.

T The way certain items will appear in this book, might seem a little different. For example, we might bring up a new topic on one page, and then connect it with something else, on another page. This jumping around will be easy for you to follow, and it will help you to remember the earlier sections of the book. It makes the information seem circular and connected. Even though the book is divided into articles and chapters, all of these sections are related to one another. They all depend on each other, to make this work. Feel free to connect certain bits of information with others, if you find there is a common thread binding them together. As you start to do this, you'll get a real sense of the book, as a whole.

H We will try to give you as much information, in as few pages, as possible.

E You won't find any famous quotes from old religious books here. The things we will be talking about will be related to them, of course, but they are common things anyway. You've heard them all before, so there's no reason for us to be repeating them.

These old sayings can help sometimes, but other times they will only make things more confusing. It depends on how you see the message. One person will see it one way, while another person sees it a different way. Which is the right one? At this point, you don't need to be wondering what something means, things should be clear and simple. Some of the messages in those old books have been written in ways that are different from how you speak and write nowadays. Haven't you seen for yourself, the amount of arguing going on about what was written in some of these books? Maybe you've even been one of the ones arguing.

Some people will claim to be experts about these books and will try to tell you what the sayings mean. They will also try to get you to believe, what they believe. The choice is yours. What do you want to believe? Do you want to listen to someone else's opinions or are you ready to finally listen to your own? In many ways, these people are just like you. You're all looking for answers.

In these times, people need a simpler way to find their answers. They seem to want the direct approach. Why "beat around the bush"? Why use fancy language to talk about something that's simple? We won't be using a lot of big words to try and impress anyone. We will do everything we can, to make this easy for you.

R If we haven't said it, then it hasn't been said by us. No reading "between the lines."

E What you call "thinking", is more like babbling to us. Your mind is constantly talking to itself. This isn't thinking. It's just something to keep you from feeling lonely or bored.

Thought, is much more natural, it just happens on its own. You don't have to think about it, it's just there. The closest thing you've seen to this is when you use your imagination. Those flashes and ideas that seem to come out of nowhere are your real thoughts. They're like a breath of fresh air; they make you feel alive. Those other so-called thoughts will leave you feeling tired and dull. This is how you can tell the difference between the two.

I We will not limit you. Please do not limit yourself.

S You will not be our victim. You have the power to choose for yourself, at all times, and in all places. It will be natural for you to feel some doubt and fear about what we're saying. This is a new experience for you. You might even worry that we will be offended if you disagree with us about something. Please don't be concerned about this. Even if you were to feel that everything we've just said is a complete and total lie; our feelings for you wouldn't change. We're not here to make you believe in anything. We've only come to give you this information.

You will decide for yourself.

O Whatever comes to you, whatever you might happen to remember, you must not be too hard on yourself. You shouldn't judge yourself.

N We won't be calling you by your human name. This is not how we see you. We don't want to place a lot of attention on the person you believe yourself to be.

Do you remember your true name?

L There is nothing to fear. No matter what you may come to see or hear, no harm will come to you. You are completely safe.

Y There is no time, other than what you're experiencing right now.

Y It's not up to us to choose the way for you, only to get you ready for the way that already exists. It's waiting for you, and we're here to help you recognize it.

O We can only help you as much as you let us. If you don't want our help, there's nothing we can do to force it upon you. This also means that when you do ask for our help, you will have to accept it the way it is. You can't change how or when it will come to you. You can't be too "picky."

U Now that you've read this far, we would like you to finish reading the book.
(There is no rush.)

Initiating *Article two*...

Article Two – Your Person

Chapter 13

Bax Here.
Did they warn you that i was coming? They probably
didn't. Well, i'm here and i would first like to say "well done",
on getting through your first lecture from *The Gathering*.
How do you like them so far? Personally, i think they tend
to go on a little. This was their big debut, and they were so
excited you found them. They really wanted to impress
you.

Sorry, if i seem critical of them. It wouldn't be right for you
to get the wrong idea. After all, we've only just met. And
you shouldn't worry that they might get angry about
anything i'm saying to you, either. There's absolutely no
chance they're insulted. This is because i just happen to
be one of them. i'm a part of *The Gathering*, and as a
member "in good standing", there can be no
misunderstandings between us. We are in constant
communication with one another. We know each other's
thoughts and feelings, at all times. With this kind of a
connection, they know when i'm teasing and when i'm
serious, and i'm rarely, ever serious. As well, because i am
one of them, anything i might happen to say about them,

i'm also saying about myself. If i'm poking fun at them, then i'm also laughing at myself. No harm done.

As you know, my name is Bax. This isn't just my name; it also tells you a little about what i'm like. My name describes me, in a way. It doesn't tell you what i am, unfortunately, but it does give you some information about my personality. If i could say it another way for you, i would say that i'm being Bax. I'm acting like Bax. Does this help at all? Don't you find that humans use their names in a similar way? Your own name for instance, can tell you a lot about your purpose in this lifetime. It's important to understand what your name means. It's not just any old name, it's a key, or a code word, that can unlock some very important information for you. It can lead to a better understanding of yourself. You may not believe me, but i have to tell you that it's true, even though your parents may not have known it, when they chose your name for you.

You've probably noticed by now, that i use the lower case of "i" when i'm talking about myself. In my world, there's only *One*, who's able to use the big "I". They don't have a name, like we do, they just use the "I." i have to be honest, aside from what i've just told you, i don't know a whole lot about the *One*. The others have asked me to tell you that, if you're interested, you can meet with the *One*, later on. Wait a minute! Actually, i've just been informed, you *will* be meeting in *Article Seven*. The big "I" has spoken.

This little "i" helps me to see my place, in the order of things. It connects me to that part of myself that still lives as an individual. That part is called Bax. When i see myself as connected with the others, i know myself as *The Gathering*. When things get more individual, then i'm being

Bax again. There are lots of ways we can think of ourselves, and each one will have its own name or way of describing itself. In your world, you might think of yourself as a person, who is also part of a larger family, and this family is part of a nation, and so on. You'll have your given names, your family name and your citizenship. Does this make more sense?

Even though my present situation is similar to yours, in that we are both on an individual level, there are some big differences. As we communicate, i won't be coming all the way into your world. i won't be human. In order to help you, it's best that i hold my position, *Here*, so that i don't get myself trapped in your world.

From what i can see, it's pretty intense over there. i wouldn't be much help to you if i became lost, as well. I'm only going far enough in, so that i can use my name and make this message seem a little more personal for you. We decided that this move, on our part, would help in forming a deeper relationship with you. It will help us to become friends!

Even though i might sound like a separate person, i'm still very much connected with *The Gathering*. Because of this, they will be the main source of all the information i will be giving you. This is to keep me from changing the information with my own opinions. In a way, i guess you could think of me as their official messenger. i am the ambassador to *The Gathering*. It's not a bad job, really.

My first task was to make the opening in your mind, a little bigger. But, it looks like you've already taken care of that, for me. This has made things easier, and it'll save us a lot of time. Before we get started on the next section, i want to thank you for making my entry into your world so easy. It took a lot of trust on your part. We understand that doing this isn't always easy for your kind and so, i will do all i can to make your efforts worthwhile.

i would like to start off by saying that i come from the Future/Past. i come from your future and our shared past. Yes, we have a past together, as well as a future; one that hasn't happened for you, yet. It's also past in the sense that realistically, all time has *Now* finished, both for you and me. We've run out of time. Where i come from, your lifetime is long gone, my friend. At the same time, my lifetime is over, too. It's all over; everything. How does this make you feel? Does it make you wonder how everything turned out in the end? Are you wondering how i'm able to talk to you if my lifetime has passed? Shouldn't i be dead or something? Any feelings and questions you're having right now are perfectly natural. It isn't everyday someone tells you that realistically, your lifetime is already over. Remember how you're feeling right now, because you're going to feel this way again.

The idea that time has disappeared, isn't always easy to swallow, no matter how thirsty you are. Think of it. As you turn your eyes away from this page, everything you see, seems to tell you the exact opposite. Life is going on all around you, and you're a part of the action. How can your lifetime be already over, when you're obviously in the middle of all this living?

Let me just remind you that what i said originally was that your lifetime was over, not that you were dead. i didn't say anything about you dying. It's a fairly common mistake, actually. After all, everything you've learned about life on Earth would seem to tell you that one day you will die. i think it would probably be a good idea for you to let go of that old way of thinking. First of all, it's a lie, and secondly you will soon be replacing that old idea with something new. After all, how could i be speaking to you, if we were both dead? Obviously, even with all of this time stuff over and done with, we haven't died. And, the fact that you can read these words, should tell you that you aren't dead. If i were a philosopher i would probably say something like, 'you read, therefore you are'. You exist in reference.

Chapter 14

As i begin to show you the truth about your life, it will probably seem like i'm making things more confusing, instead of clearer. It'll look like i'm making things worse, instead of better. Please believe me when i say that i've come to improve things, for you. But, in order to do this, i'm going to have to turn your world upside down for a while. This is one of the side-effects of the process. If it'll make you feel any better, i can tell you that it'll only be temporary. It won't last long.

No matter what, it's important for me to finish what i've started. It wouldn't do either of us any good if i was to only do part of the job, and then leave you to clean up the mess. Any trust i may have earned with you, would instantly be gone. Who knows how long it would take for us to get hold of your attention, again. We could lose you for a very long time.

The adjustment stage will be a little uncomfortable, at first, but as you start to move yourself out of this confusion, you'll begin to feel a whole lot better. It's important that you learn the truth about your life, as soon as possible; for your sake and for the benefit of those around you. i will do everything i can to make this as clear as possible, because it will affect everything else from this point on. If we can go back to what i said earlier, i'll say it this way:

Your lifetime may be over, but your *Life* is not.

Even though they're closely related, a person's lifetime and their Life are two different things. The first one is limited, while the other isn't. A lifetime has a beginning and an end, while *Life* simply, goes on....

My dear, everything you see, hear and touch; all of this around you, is not your *Life*, it's only a lifetime. It's just a small part of what your *Life* really is. Have you ever felt that, "there must be more to life" than this? Well, you can bet on it! There is more to *Life*; much, much more. And, it's just waiting for you to find it. This might be hard for you to realize right now, but in terms of your *Life*, you are so much more than you could possible imagine! You are much more than you seem to be. i'm so excited! It's like i've been carrying around this incredible secret about you, and finally i'm able to let you in on it! Very soon, you're going to be busy with learning to see the differences between your *Life*, and this lifetime. As it gets clearer, you will discover a wonderful, hidden surprise and, in realizing it, you will have taken the first step toward the *Reference Point*. This little treasure, is the answer to the greatest of all human mysteries, searched for by countless men and women, since the beginning of civilization. This first step is, by far, the greatest challenge you'll have to face in *Reality*. All the others that follow will seem like "child's play." You're very close to this first step, and it is a "doozie."

We'll start off with a simple question. i'd like you to think about it, and give yourself an honest answer. Feel free to take as long as you like.

Is this lifetime on Earth, actually real?

My star pupil, it is my responsibility to remind you that everything is not what it seems. What you think might be happening, isn't really happening. Although there's a part of it that is real, the rest is totally and completely false. It's a sham, a trick. i'm sorry if this has put you into shock. i am trying to break the news as gently as possible. Sometimes there's just no easy way to say these things. As i said before, this early stage can be a little difficult to handle. After all, you're seeing it all in front of you right now, and everything about it tells you that it's real. You can see it, touch it, smell it, and it feels real to you. You can talk with the others in your world, and they seem real too. You have everything you need to prove it to yourself, right? You've suffered pain and hunger, as well as having enjoyed all sorts of good times with friends and family. But, even with all of this, there's still that feeling that there must be something more. Somehow all of this, never seems to be enough.

i don't want you to actually do anything about what i've just told you. It's better to move carefully, during these early stages. For now, it's enough that i've said it. Maybe it was too much. Understanding it all, will come as you move through the process and learn more about your surroundings. For now, try not to look as if anything has upset you. Just pretend that you're reading an average, everyday book, (that doesn't really exist) so that no one will suspect anything strange is going on.

If all of these earthly adventures aren't actually real, then what's really going on? Do you remember what we told you, back in *Article One*? What you're experiencing is something you call "Reality". Let me welcome you to the show! If you'll just humor me for a few minutes, i'm going to be using your powers of imagination to help show you some of the incredible features of this place.

Chapter 15

Once upon a time, there were clear instructions for how to get *Home*. This was provided for any who might have gotten lost in *Reality*. These instructions included the story of *Reality*, along with some clear pointers for leaving. These signs were carefully placed, so that anyone could find them. They were literally written in stone, so they would last.

Throughout time, however, there have been certain persons who knew the truth about *Reality*, didn't want to go *Home* and didn't want anyone else to leave, either. As a result, they did all they could to have this helpful information buried or completely destroyed. No one was ever supposed to find the truth; no one was ever supposed to leave. They were unsuccessful. Sections of these instructions have been found recently and are being kept safe, but there are still others that remain hidden.

Hidden doesn't mean lost.

There have always been those among you who could see the truth. And even though they knew the way *Home*, they stayed to share what they knew. They worked to preserve the truth, even if it meant hiding some of it. If they hid the truth, it was only to protect it from being lost. They knew that others would one day be needing it, others like you. They also knew that saving the truth might be dangerous for them, but they didn't worry. Having figured out *Reality*, they knew that even if their lifetime was to be suddenly cut short, their *Life* would continue.

The pieces that have been found, along with the advice of the ones who know the truth in your lifetime, will be very helpful in the times ahead. But they won't be enough to get you *Home*. The rest will come from you. You are very important in this process. Soon you'll begin discovering bits and pieces of the truth on your own. You won't believe in it at first, but eventually the clues you find will prove themselves to you. You'll begin to trust them; you'll begin to trust in yourself.

When this happens, you'll begin to notice that you aren't as worried all the time; you aren't so afraid. Things will start to seem just fine. There are clues all around you. *Reality* is here, now, right in front of you. Everything you need to know is right before your eyes. It's literally built-in to the framework of *Reality*. Once your eyes become adjusted to a new way of seeing things, the answers will become as "plain as day". You'll wonder how you ever missed them. The truth can never really be hidden or destroyed. That idea was so misguided. Now that we're in contact again, the process will move along more quickly.

We're going to be using *Reality* to get you *Home*. We aren't going to fight against *Reality*. It's going to be our friend, in a way. Without realizing it, it's going to be helping us. Because *Reality* is like a machine, it doesn't mind if we use it to get you safely *Home*. It won't even realize what we're doing, because it's too busy following instructions.

In the beginning, the *Reality* designers shared little more, than their hopes of discovering some new form of entertainment. They wanted to create the ultimate alternative to a *Life* of complete freedom. After all, how much could One stand? It just went on forever! But, their hopes for creating such a lifestyle weren't possible in any *real* way, so they came up with the idea of building it through a "make-believe" one. In order to make it work, we would need to pretend. They'd make-up a fake world for everyone, with all kinds of characters, adventures, money, and so on. This was pretty darn clever, if they did say so themselves. (And they did.) No one had ever thought to try such a thing before -- how radical! How could One be so bold! Comments aside, it didn't take long before everyone wanted to give this little *Reality* a try.

The rules for the *Reality* experience are simple. As the player chooses to go into this experience, they must agree to follow the rules of the program. There are many programs to choose from, and each one has certain rules regarding what you're able to do while you're in that program. There's no limit to your choice of program, but there are limits within those choices. Once you decide on the one you want, you have to take it the way it is. If you were to try and change it, you would upset the other players and ruin all the fun.

Once you've settled on a program, and have gone into it, you can't change your mind. At that point, it's too late. You can, however, choose to avoid certain parts of the program, from time to time. It's a lot like saying "pass" when your turn comes up. You're still in the game, you've just chosen not to make your move at that time. This is the only exception, as it doesn't cause any major changes to the program. It's a brief pause in the game, that's all. You can plan to complete the turn at another point in time, but it must be completed, in all fairness to the others. They don't tell you how to complete your turn, just that you do it.

**"No one may leave the game,
until all moves have been completed."**

Reality has been specially designed to avoid any disturbances between your program and those of the others. They will all be interacting with one another, so it would be best if everything ran smoothly. Oh yes, didn't i tell you? There are many others enjoying themselves in this place, and they might be upset if you were to suddenly decide that you wanted to leave. Their programs depend on yours, and yours depends on theirs. Each of you plays a part in completing one another's programs. Refusing to follow through with your part would, in time, cause major problems. The others would have to wait for you to act, before they could go on with their parts. (We recently found an exception, or "loophole" to this rule. We'll be dealing with this further-on, and you'll realize how it can help.)

The rule of having to wait for someone to complete their turn has created some problems lately. A lot of players are taking too long to finish their moves. Because of this, the designers decided to allow for "stand-ins". If you can find someone else who's willing to play certain parts for you, then this will help to let the others move on. The idea of switching players for parts, has worked well up to this point, but there's a catch. These aren't real substitutions. You will still need to eventually make your move. Also, in asking someone else to help you out, you now owe them a favor. You will have to play a part for them one day, and you may not like the one they choose for you. As you're beginning to see, things can get pretty complicated. It's best to just play your part when your turn comes up. After all, you *did* agree to it.

Of course, you couldn't possibly remember agreeing to any of these conditions, because of this next rule. "Upon entering the *Reality* program, all players will instantly give up all knowledge of their true *Self*. They will forget everything." It's quite surprising to many of you, just how intense and complete this process of forgetting can really be. It can actually make *One* believe that they have become an entirely new person. The guest of *Reality* now believes that they are someone else.

Upon arrival, there is a bright "flash" of light. All memories are set aside. *Reality* is now in control. Then comes the terrible confusion and you begin to fall. Helpless and without a point of reference, there is no choice but to give-in to the movement of *Reality*. In order to survive, you must now follow *its* ways. You are now dependent. It sounds very bad, but let's not forget that it's just for fun. It's not really happening. Your loss of memory is only temporary. Unfortunately, no one can remember this. It was set up this way, so that you could really enjoy your *Reality* experience. Having forgotten who and what you actually are, you can then really, be this new person. You can become totally involved in this new world, with nothing, to hold you back. There's no denying, it's a crucial part of being able to make all of this work. It gives you the opportunity for a fresh start, every time.

There are some parts to this memory feature that aren't so appealing. It seems to have produced some unexpected complications in those who've returned from their visits. But, even with these side-effects, there's an incredible waiting list for anyone wanting to get in. They know about the memory loss, they've witnessed the confusion and the fear, still, there seems to be nothing we can do to stop them.

It would appear, this make-believe world is a bit too believable. It has drawn you in, gotten hold of your attention and formed an attachment with you. Having gone through countless sessions, without a single break, there are many of you who've lost your sense of what's true. When you came to the end of your program, you always decided to stay and play. When the bell rang to tell you that the game was over, you just turned around and started a new one. You're probably wondering why no one made you stop. This is the tough part. You see, it's not allowed. We can't make you do anything. You have free will, remember? Apart from *Reality*, you are free to do whatever you like. If you want to live in the *Reality* experience, that's entirely up to you. Once you've made your decision, we have to respect it. Every time you came out of your experience, there was always someone there to say, "Awaken friend and remember who you are. It was all just a dream; a little game, and now it is over". But, you didn't want to believe them, you always wanted, "one more time". So, off you went. We could see what all of this was doing to you, but we couldn't help. You didn't *want* our help, you wanted *Reality*.

In the beginning, you had no trouble leaving the *Reality* experience. At the end of your session, you would appear and instantly remember your real *Self*. There was never any problem, and you always had a lot to say about your experiences. It was the same for everyone. From inside *Reality*, going *Home* was originally seen as the "death" event. When a person "died," their program was over. For some, this happened at a young age, and for others it happened later. But they were all just leaving the game. They weren't really dead. Unfortunately, this wouldn't last for long. Those of you who went in, again and again, gradually began to lose control. When you "died" and came *Home*, you didn't see it as such, and ran back to the only home you knew; *Reality*. It became your new home. As a result, the "death" event began to have no effect upon ending your stay in *Reality*. When you "died", you just automatically went back-in for another lifetime of experience. There was no way for you to recognize when the game was over, or when you had finished your part. It looks like you got your wish. You could now stay as long as you liked, and you never had to come *Home*. *Reality* has now grown to include the "death" event as part of its program. It's not the "way-out" it once was, millions of years ago. You've been playing for a very long time, my friend.

Adding this option has really made way for an incredible expansion of the *Reality* experience. There are now all kinds of new programs to choose from; the largest and most impressive of these being, *The Dimensions of the Dead*. The Earth selection, as diverse as it is, can only offer you a small part of the total list of possibilities. You can send your thanks for this creative leap, to the incredible power of desire.

Chapter 16

When you first began to see the others dying in your world, you didn't pay much attention. Death was a 'fact of life', a natural part of living in this world. Of course, you felt something when they did die, but this feeling eventually went away. Survival was difficult in the beginning; it was all you could do to stay alive.

As time moved on, things got better; you were able to live longer and enjoy more experiences. You got to know the others a little more and formed connections with them. You started to feel many things when the others were around. Some of the things you felt were good, and some of them were not. It was strange for you to feel one way, one minute, then another way, the next. There wasn't much you could do about it. These feelings were alive and they seemed to come to you whenever they wanted. You had to accept them. Longer lifetimes and ever deepening relationships eventually became quite common in your world, and it was at this point in your history when the death event seriously began to bother you. "What happens to the others, once they've stopped moving and turned cold? What happened to the light in their eyes?" So many questions started to burn within the minds of those who lived on. What was happening to their friends and family? "Have they gone to another place? Is this all there is to this lifetime; to struggle and then die? Does it really end this way?" Of course, no one wanted to believe that this was *really* the end, so they began to think of what the possibilities might be. If they were to leave this life, where would they go? What would they do?

Relying on dreams and using their imaginations, those who worked to uncover this great mystery brought new hope to the ones who were left behind. You never needed to look very far to find someone with an opinion on this subject. Given so many possibilities, there were often disagreements over who's version was more likely to be true. This put a fair amount of pressure on people to come up with some kind of proof for their ideas. When proof was hard to find, people did the next best thing to try and sell their theory. They used persuasion and intimidation.

Eventually, certain stories about the after-death were agreed on and seemed to be tailor-made to suit the lifestyles of those living within the different regions of your planet. They were important stories. They gave the people something to believe in, something to hope for, as they struggled through their difficult lifetimes. Without these stories, things would've seemed unbearable for them. As you can imagine, the idea of a person's whole life ending as a cold lump of rotting flesh, didn't seem very attractive. There had to be something more; some kind of reward for all of the struggle and the pain of this living.

Over time, the power of these stories grew. They became legends. Visions of the after-death became clearer, more realistic for all of you. You wouldn't need to wonder anymore. At last a person could be sure of something! It was quite a relief. In the minds of the people, these stories were alive. They weren't just mythical tales; they were real. They were the truth. And this my friend, was how *The Dimensions of the Dead* were created. The designers simply borrowed these stories of the after-death, from the minds of those within *Reality* so that they could have what they most wanted.

"The customer is always right!"

All of you were there when it happened. You were *all* responsible. This was something all of you wanted, and you wanted it very badly. Who could refuse you?

Here are your new instructions for the death event in this lifetime:

"After completing the death event, all players will go to that area, where they believe they are destined. The direction of their thoughts, at the time of death, will instantly guide them to that place."

Sorry about the legal tone of that one. This is basically the ticket to your next lifetime, and it's built-in to your program, so you don't need to worry about having to do something extra. It doesn't care if you've completed all of your moves for this lifetime or not. You can always come back and finish them later. Remember, dying doesn't signal the end of your program anymore. If you don't finish all of your moves in this lifetime, you can do so in the next, or in the one after that. It's all up to you, but they *do* need to be completed. And, with this rule in place, you don't need to visit *The Dimensions of the Dead*, if you don't want to. Those dimensions won't help you to complete your original moves anyway because they showed up after you we're already in *Reality*. They're optional.

i'm sure this all sounds pretty straightforward in many ways, but as you might have noticed, there's a problem. How are you supposed to know which moves actually need finishing? Who will be interacting with you, in order to complete those moves? How are you to know when it's time to make them? The little details of your program were forgotten a long time ago, and since dying no longer signals the end of your session, you're pretty much left with "trial and error." You're making all these moves, wondering, "Is this the right choice?", or "Am I doing the right thing?" Can you really know, for sure? There's always going to be some doubt, in everything you do. This is really turning out to be a lot of guesswork for everyone, and it's not much fun anymore. If only you could figure out what needs to be done, so that you could finish the game.

There's no use looking for someone to blame for this situation. Everyone is responsible for what happened. There's no sense in feeling guilty or angry about it either, because these feelings won't help you. Let's just keep working together and i assure you that all of these problems will eventually be taken care of. Trust me, there is another way out of this place.

Chapter 17

The fact that you can't seem to remember who you really are, doesn't mean that there's something wrong with you. At the same time, you're not weak or useless, just because you've fallen into this little mess. The very thing that's happened to you, has also happened to everyone else. You're not alone. You're all in this together.

As you're reading this, however, there are some, who've managed to find their way. Although they aren't actually "out" yet, they're definitely very close. The secrets to your leaving this place are not impossible for you to figure-out. They were never meant to be. This was never meant to be some kind of trap for you. You were never meant to stay here this long. The ones who have learned the secrets of *Reality*, were no different from you, at this stage. They had to go through all of the same things you're experiencing, in order to get where they are now. It's all part of the process, and if they were able to do it, so can you.

What was their secret? Basically, they discovered the true nature of *Reality*. They learned to see through all of the "magic" and the "mirrors", to what was really behind all of this. What they found was something truly wonderful, and it surprised them. You see, what happened was, they *remembered*. It was only a little, at first, but it still happened. It was a small step, but it was in the right direction. Please don't think that they were special or "super human" in some way, because they weren't. And, they wouldn't want you to think of them in that way. It would only create a distance between you, at a time when they need you to come closer. Essentially, they're just a number of moves ahead of you in the game, that's all. You'll soon catch-up to them.

In order to help you catch-up, i'm going to let you in on three little secrets. The secrets themselves, are very simple to understand. The hard part is in actually beginning to use them. This is because you're not used to doing things, or seeing things in the way that i'm about to show you. At first, it's going to seem like a lot of work, but later you'll see how the old way of doing things was actually much harder. One way to make it easier on yourself, and everyone else, is for you to actually *want* to do it. It was your longing, or your desire, which first brought you into this place, and so, you will need to use this same longing, to get you out. You'll have to actually want to leave, or it just won't work.

What i'm about to do, is simply remind you of something that was said earlier. It won't surprise you to read it, but i feel that it's important enough to justify repeating. It's crucial that you, first, accept your *Reality* for what it is; a fantasy, a magical "trick", a game. The first thing you will need to realize is:

Everything i'm experiencing is like a dream.

Everything, every person and all that happens within *Reality*, is make-believe. It's fiction, and that's probably what it says on the liner of this book, too. Now, this doesn't mean that it isn't real. Please, don't get me wrong. There's still a bit of truth hidden deep within everything that surrounds you. It's just a question of finding it. Now, to help you in your search, i'm going to tell you what that bit of truth is. It's known as *the cause*. The cause of everything you experience in this world, is real. This is what really matters. The rest is just part of the show. That's all i'm going to say about this, for now.

Regarding the second secret, you may remember when i spoke of a "loophole" to one of the rules of *Reality*. At that time, we were talking about how important it was for you to complete your part in the program. i also said that the others might be angry, if you were to suddenly decide that you wanted to leave the game. Well, as it turns out, they might be offended, or they might not. They have a choice. There's no rule that says they have to feel a certain way. In fact, if they wanted to, they could even release you from the game, altogether. You would be finished playing; there wouldn't be any leftover moves for you to complete. Your program would be over, and you would be Free! Wouldn't this be nice of them? In the same breath, you could just as easily release someone else from their part, in your program; helping to send them *Home*. There's no law that says you have to force them to play their part. Arrangements can be re-arranged. You can let them go.

What do you think? It sounds pretty simple, doesn't it? As i've said, these secrets are easy to understand, but putting them into action, takes a little work. In this particular case, there's some "fine print" you'll need to understand. First of all, the game has grown so large, and become so complicated, that the chances of everyone releasing one another from their parts, all at the same time, are pretty slim. There is, thankfully, such a thing as partial release; which would definitely speed up the process; even if you didn't get out as fast as you'd hoped. Secondly, no matter how badly you might want to help the others by releasing them, they might not want this help. Not everyone is interested in leaving at this time. Many of the others have come here to play certain roles and parts in the game, and they have every right to do so. No one can force them to leave. They'll go, when they're ready. Now, for the one's that *are* ready to leave, there's the question of how to go about releasing them.

Let's continue the process by saying:

i am now ready to finish the game.
i welcome any release from my part, in the playing.
i release all others, from the demands of my program.
i am ready to go *Home*.

This statement is powerful enough to end the game, right now. But, in order for this to happen, everyone and everything would have to say it, and they would have to really mean it. Actually, the statement's power comes from you; all of you. Without you, it's worthless; just a bunch of meaningless words. *You* are the key, to making it work.

Now, there's no need for you to go around repeating it, over and over, like a broken record. And, you certainly don't need to memorize it. Actually, you only needed to say it, this once. And, now, you've done it. You've helped with the process of returning. There is someone or something "out there", that needed you to say it, even this once. They may not even be completely aware of what it means for them, but for some reason their lifetime just became a little easier to handle. That huge load they were carrying, suddenly got a little lighter. A time will come, when they will feel that they need to "do" something, and then that feeling will suddenly disappear. They won't have to do it anymore, because you've let them go. In some way, they'll know that it was you who did this, and it will change the way they feel about you. They will remember you.

Chapter 18

One of the odd things about your journey *Home*, is that you never can tell what will happen next. Even though your whole lifetime has been completely planned out for you, the next few moments will always remain a collection of mysterious unknowns. Oh sure, you're probably thinking that in the next few moments you'll simply be reading from these pages and nothing spectacular will happen. But, what if it did? Would you be ready for it? This world can be full of surprises; some wonderful and others, not so much.

Nothing, in your world ever stays the same. It's constantly changing. And, because of all this change, you will often find that little surprises interrupt your plans for a smooth ride in this lifetime. No matter what you do to avoid them, they manage to find you. You'll take better care of yourself, you'll organize your daily activities and still there's always a little something that rubs you the wrong way, or gets in the way of your plans. The day never seems quite right, no matter how well you've set things up. These little surprises can start to pile-up, especially in your modern way of living.

You're exposed to a lot of living in these times and you open yourself up to a lot more possibilities for surprise. You see, it works on a percentage basis; if you lead a simpler life, the number of surprises decreases from the faster and more complex sort of lifestyle. The lower numbers of surprises are easier for you to handle; they don't tend to wear you out so much. But, as they start to increase for you, you can really see the difference it makes. Sometimes these extra surprises can be exciting and make you feel more alive, and this can be a good experience for you. But, it would be best if they weren't happening at these higher levels on a daily basis. i believe when this happens, you call it "stress."

As i look at your situation, it seems that there's not a lot you can do right now to try and decrease the number of surprises your receiving on a daily basis. So, i won't be asking you to make any changes in this respect, but i would like to offer you a way of getting ready for these surprises, so that they're less surprising for you. i want to try and soften their impact on your life; moving them from a slap to a tickle, if i may.

When you look into the future what do you see? You see many things; many possibilities of what may come your way. Then, the process of choosing begins; the possibilities you would like to happen, from the ones you would like to avoid. The ones to be avoided are put away, as far away as possible, and may even be forgotten for a while. You focus upon the ones you want, and hope that these are the ones coming your way. But, you can't be sure if they'll come or not. All you can do is hope. How do things usually turn-out?

Oftentimes, things just don't seem to turn-out they way you had hoped they would. You might be thinking that you've had pretty good luck with this style of planning for the future, but that's probably because you tend to remember the times you won, over the times you lost. This helps to keep you going, but it's not based on anything you can really use to help your situation. There is a better way, that can improve the odds in your favor.

As i look into your future, i need to warn you that it will be bringing many, new challenges. When they come, you will be given the chance to see them in a number of different ways. Make sure your eyes are open. These challenges are meant to be enjoyable, but you may not choose to see them this way. If you could see them for what they really are, you would know that they're just another part of your program; the reason you're here, remember? You would see their real purpose; which is, to entertain you. They're supposed to be fun challenges. Some of them are harder than others, i won't argue with that, but there's plenty of help all around you. Just ask.

There's a simple way to get ready for these challenges. It was discovered a long time ago by one of those who've managed to find their way. It comes from their own experiences in *Reality*, and they've asked me to pass it on to you.

THE EXPECTED

Do not look to another for happiness.
Do not look to me.
For i will always disappoint you,
and your expectations of me.

Living up to these expectations...
i cannot,
nor do i wish,
nor is it my purpose (to do so).

All i shall ever ask,
expect me only,
as i do you,
as ... *The Unexpected*.

The *Expected* is something that exists in your world. It's not a person, but it is alive. It's been having a lot of trouble lately, because everyone seems to be depending on it a bit too much. This is pushing it beyond its capabilities. It's not designed to take-on this much responsibility. The

Expected is doing its very best to make everything work-out for you the way you want it to be, but it can't keep up. The *Expected* needs some help from you. It needs for you to think of it in a new way; as the *Unexpected*. This is what it was meant to be, but somehow it ended up becoming the *Expected* instead. Now, it's not telling you what to expect from your life, that's for you to choose, but it is telling you how to go about expecting it. There is a difference.

Everyone has expectations. It's important to be able to plan for the future. Your lifetime has to move in some sort of direction; and in planning it, you'll need to imagine just what you want that future to look like. i'm not trying to tell you that it's wrong to have these expectations, i just think it would be better if you didn't depend on them too much. Maybe it would be better to start thinking of them as possibilities; things that might happen for you. As you've seen many times already, this is much closer to what they really are anyway. Sometimes they happen and sometimes they don't. Do you really want to put all of your hopes into the *Expected*? Do you honestly believe that it's reliable enough, that you can depend on it with your life? Because, that's exactly what this comes down to.

Expecting the *Expected* as the *Unexpected* can be a lot like receiving a wonderfully wrapped present. You have no idea what's inside, but you're still happy when it comes. You just can't wait to unwrap it and see what's inside. It's like being a kid again. Can you remember? There are many of you, however, who would rather not open the present, at all. Not knowing what's inside can be a very uncomfortable feeling. If only you could be sure of what was inside, before you opened it. Then you could enjoy it. That would be okay. But, while a person is "humming and hawing," the present suddenly disappears. It's gone. We will have no way of ever knowing what was waiting inside. It could have been just what you've always wanted; the answer to all of your hopes.

Surprise is a strange thing to get used to. It leaves many of you with mixed feelings. In some ways it's very exciting, and in other ways it's pretty scary. Are these feelings both the same thing? All of the planning and organizing, in order to avoid being surprised is fairly hopeless anyway. The surprises still happen. And, some of the surprises are disappointing because you were expecting something better. Is it really worth going to all the trouble? Why not just let the surprises come, in their own time, and in their own way? They're going to anyway, right? Can you really hope to control the *Unexpected*? No. All you can do is expect it. When you're expecting the *Expected*, you're only ready for one or, maybe two things to happen, that's it. With the *Unexpected*, you're now ready for just about anything, and believe me, anything is the very thing for which you'll need to be ready.

"Expect only the Unexpected."

Let me ask you a couple of simple questions. When you first saw my name at the start of this article, where you surprised? Did you expect *The Gathering* to continue speaking? Was i unexpected, or were you maybe given a hint that i might be on the way? If you did expect me, what did you expect me to be like? Am i what you thought?

Let's imagine, for a moment, that you've made plans to meet with a friend. For some reason, they didn't show-up according to plan. How do you feel? Are you hurt, angry, or surprised? Do you feel like you've wasted your time, coming to this place, where no one is here to meet you? i'm not here to judge your feelings, we're just imagining together. Please be honest with yourself.

While you were imagining all of this, did it ever cross your mind that these plans could be happening for some other reason; different from the one you thought? Maybe, you weren't actually supposed to meet with them, after all. What if there was another plan, one going on behind the scenes, to have you be in a certain place and time for other, unknown reasons. Has this ever happened to you? Have you ever gone somewhere to do one thing, and found yourself doing something else, something that turned out to be more important? Maybe your being there was for the sake of another, someone you didn't even know. It could have been as simple as being there to give someone directions, when they were lost. It was a simple thing, but it meant a lot. And, it was completely unexpected.

Finally, (because i know you want to get to the end of this chapter), i would like to ask that you not expect too much from yourself. After all, this is a beginning; you're just getting started. Expect the *Unexpected* from yourself, too. Allow yourself to be surprised *by* yourself. It can be a lot of fun actually, being able to make yourself laugh, to feel good about something you "all of a sudden" did for someone, and to sometimes feel moved to tears by a small act of kindness from someone else.

These are precious moments.

Try not to worry too much about the 'road' ahead. Everything is moving along really well from where i'm seeing it. i don't need to remind you that worrying will wear you out. When you find that certain things and people are starting to get you down, just ask yourself: "Will i still be worrying about this tomorrow? or next week? or, even next year?" Your problems are not you, and because of this, they're nothing. One day, you'll forget all about the problems you're facing today. That time is equally the same as *Now*.

Don't ever feel that you should be in a 'rush' to get *Home*. This isn't some kind of race that you need to win. Everyone's a winner in *The End*. We've organized things so that your journey will move along at a more relaxed pace. This will help to avoid any sudden shock, which might lead to fear. You have all the time you need to get things done. Also, time and space aren't what they seem to be. If you could see just how simple they actually are, you would understand why i've said to you that 'there is no rush'. We'll be passing along more than a few secrets, and some of these will deal with the truth about time and space.

We know that you're still enjoying yourself in a lot of ways, so we've decided to focus on using the things you enjoy, to bring you *Home* to us. We will use the rules of your program to their own end. i wouldn't want you to feel as if you needed to sacrifice anything.

i've come to bring you back from all this daydreaming, or *Dreaming of Days*, as we call it. i'm here to help set your mind at ease about the lifetime you're living. Looking back on it, i want to let you know that it was a great success! Unfortunately, this is all i can say about it, right now. i'm not allowed to get into the details. If i did, it would interfere with your freedom. The information might cheat you out of many wonderful experiences. And, part of the 'wonder' involves them being a surprise for you. We wouldn't want to ruin all the fun, now would we? Please don't be angry with me. In time, i hope you'll see that it was 'all for the best'.

Chapter 19

Moving into this next chapter, we'll be exploring a few questions. These questions are fairly well known to you and the others. If you want, you can think of them as the next step in moving towards your *Reference Point*. You can start by asking yourself these two simple questions...

Who am i?
What am i?

At this stage, you have a pretty good idea of who and what you seem to be. But, is that all there is? Do you sometimes feel like there's a little more to you than "meets the eye"?

Part of getting to know the real you involves getting to know this person you've become. Why is it that you do and say certain things the way you do? Why do you like some things and hate others? Why do you get angry, or sad? And, where do all these feelings come from, anyway? How did you manage to become the person you see in the mirror? This is the perfect time for you to be completely honest with your self. After all, nobody else really needs to know the answers to these questions, but you. If you want to share these answers with someone else that's fine, but you don't need to. It won't affect the success of your journey *Home*, either way. These answers are just for you. It's important that you try to find the answers to these questions. You're going to be hearing from some other personalities soon, and i want you to know that their opinions won't always agree with yours. No matter what they say, i want you to hold on to your *own* ideas. These personalities are designed to keep you in *Reality*. *Reality* is not your *Home*. i'll be letting these personalities speak through me. They have some helpful information that we can use. Their voices do not belong to *the Gathering*; they never have. They are the voices of *Reality*. i'll be acting as a 'bridge' between you and them. At the same time, i'll be trying my best to avoid getting pulled-in to your world. These voices know a lot about the world. They can help you learn a lot about the person you think you are. They can also answer questions about *Reality*. Going *Home* means becoming a bit of an expert on *Reality*. In your own way, you'll learn to master it.

From this point on, except for the voice of *The One*, any new personalities you happen to meet in this article, will be speaking to you from different parts of *Reality*. The voices might remind you of certain people, but they aren't actual persons. They're more like tendencies, or qualities within some of you. Because of this, they aren't complete. They're like little pieces of the puzzle, not the "big picture." When you meet them, they won't actually know that they're talking with you. They won't know they're helping you. They'll give you a point of view, their way of seeing the world. They can be helpful when it comes to making personal choices. As you move through your days, you'll begin to notice that you form a kind of partnership with them. You will sometimes need to see things the way they do, but it will only be temporary. Their truth is not your truth. They're only here for you as tools.

It's time to build the bridge. Remember that these voices are speaking through me and that i am always between the two of you. Know that i will stop them from speaking if any problems come up. No matter how difficult it is for you to believe this, you are ready to receive this information. Here goes....

Chapter 20

Your Body is Awake

My name is Babb. The many new and unusual sensations you are now experiencing, come from a unique experience known as *The Body Sensual*. We'll admit, it's quite unlike the reality of your true Self, but in this one finds an opportunity for something completely different. Isn't this the very reason you've come? Take a few moments to get better acquainted with this body of yours. It will be time well spent.

Explore your connection to this body. Your relationship with your body is one of possession. This means you are living in your body. This statement shouldn't actually surprise you too much, for this is what you've accepted all along. But, do you also realize that your body has a mind of its own as well? Yours isn't the only opinion floating around in this body, you know. You should not think of this body as being *who* you are. The body is a specially designed means for achieving all that you've hoped to experience in this lifetime. Think of your body as a possession, something "to have and to hold, until death do you both part." Think of this body as a friend. It will be your partner through all that you've chosen to suffer and enjoy. This friend can be extremely helpful and should be respected for this ability. Please don't think of it as being separate from you, or less than you. While you're immersed within *Reality*, it will be your only chance of successfully returning *Home*. Always remember this. i will now stand aside and allow your body to share some of its secrets with you. Listen carefully; can you hear it speaking?

i am your body, the way you are able to experience the world of the senses. All that you encounter of this world shall be through me. i will be your personal guide and protector. Your experience of this world will not be complete in every way, for i am limited in my abilities to translate the whole of *Reality* to you. Do not let this discourage you however, for our time together will be like nothing you have ever known. In order that your stay may be everything you had hoped, i have prepared a small list of recommendations that should help you in getting along with the others.

First, i would like to speak to you about communicating with these others. Sending messages is a slow and imperfect process in this world, and so i would ask for your patience. Choose your words and the tone of these words carefully, in your mind. Place me in such a way that the message you hope to send to someone else, matches with the overall shape of how i look to them. There is something called "Body Language" in this world. It works when the two of us are in sync, and it doesn't work so well when we're not. i really want to help you, but you've got to keep me informed of what you want to say. This way, your words won't be saying one thing while i'm showing another. Does this make sense to you? Many of the others are really good at reading 'Body Language' and they know when something isn't quite right. When we're out of sync with one another, the others are not likely to pay much attention to your messages. They may even ignore you.

Secondly, i don't appreciate it when you compare me to other bodies. i will remind you that i have been designed to fulfill all the requirements of your visit to this world. Everything that you hope to accomplish has been included in my design. i am everything you need for a successful lifetime with the assurance of returning *Home*. Don't worry too much about how all these bodies look. It's important to remember that you are not your body. i am your body. When you think about wanting another kind of body, you're confusing this very point. You're thinking that i am you. i am not. If someone should happen to make the same mistake of confusing us, one for the other, please remind them that you are not what you appear to be, nor are they. Don't worry that i might be insulted by anyone's disapproval of how i might look. As i've already said, i am perfect in every way. There were no mistakes made, in my creation. Thirdly, you will notice that i am easily trained in performing all kinds of routine tasks. This kind of training helps me to develop habits. These can be handy sometimes, when you want me to do something without too much thought from you. i will do it automatically for you and i'm happy to do so, if it will make your lifetime more enjoyable. Please remember that these little habits were once learned and so can easily be unlearned. As well, not all of these little habits are good for me. Please remember this when you are deciding on whether or not to give me some new habit. i won't always say when i'm unhappy about something you do to me, because i want you to have a good time. i want you to be happy with me. i do have a breaking point however, and when you push me too far, i'm afraid i'm going to have to push back a little. Otherwise, you won't be able to complete all that you had hoped in this lifetime. If i didn't push back, you'd end up cutting your time here a little short. (if you know what i mean.)

i must remind you that you are the one in control. i can help you out if you'll let me, but for the most part, you're in charge of taking good care of us. You'll be making the important choices and i'll be doing what i can, to help you carry them through.

Because we bodies are each "one of a kind," it's probably best you don't follow a generalized approach to my care. Try certain things and see what works best. i'll let you know what i like and what i don't like. When something doesn't sit well with me you'll know fairly soon, because i'll be doing my darnedest to get rid of whatever it is you've given me. (and i can think of two or three possible exit points for this) When i do this, please remember what it was you tried giving me, and stay away from it.

Something unusual about your being here, is our need for sleep. Actually, i'm the only one who needs the rest, but you'll be the one feeling tired when I do need this break.

Now i've heard that this isn't something you normally do, where you're from, so it might take some getting used to. For your own good, i must tell you that bodies need rest; anyhow, anyway. If you happen to have selected a Modern time frame, you no doubt have noticed how preoccupied everyone is with relaxing. Now, relaxing is different from resting. Relaxing is for the mind and resting is for me. If it's early in the day and you feel tired, but can't quite figure-out why, then it's likely you need to relax. Relaxing isn't some in-between stage between moving around and being asleep. Relaxing involves doing some simple task like walking or gardening, that doesn't require you to do a whole lot of thinking. To properly relax, pick something that i can do automatically, and let me do it. i'm not real sure how the process works, but it does. Don't sit around if you want to relax, do something, but something simple. Sitting around makes me restless and sore. i generally like to be doing something, or sleeping. Pick one, or the other and we will both feel a whole lot better.

As a final note, i would like to remind you that everything you experience while in this body has been filtered through me. There is no direct, or first hand experience when you are living inside me. All the information you receive, is brought to you by someone or something else. Should you trust this information? That will be up to you. My eyes, ears, skin, etc. are designed to provide you with certain, select bits of information. It is from this second-hand experience that you will be making all the important choices in your lifetime. These bits of coded information are like little clues. They secretly hold all the answers to the mysteries of this world. Working together, you and i shall solve these mysteries, revealing a hidden wealth, lying at the heart of their discovery!

Chapter 21

Welcome back! I hope you enjoyed your visit with Babb and *The Body Sensual*. This is Bax, again. Let's take a short break from the voices to explain a few things.

As you've just read, this body is yours, but it's not you. You're so much more. For instance, let's think of the real you as being a huge tree, and the person you think you are, as just one small leaf on this tree. This leaf is a small, but important part of the whole tree. Your human body knows how this relationship works. It knows that it has grown from you, that it will help to nourish you, and that it will one day fall away when the time is right. The real you is personally connected to this "leaf," to your human body. When you decided to make this connection, you chose to focus upon this one little part of your self, forgetting the rest. You've forgotten about all the other "leaves" on the tree. These others are an equally important part of your *Life*. You don't need to worry about this, it's part of the process of entering *Reality*. In order to successfully join in the game, you had to put them aside for a little while. i'm here to remind you that these other parts of you still exist. Your body knows that it's a part of you and not the other way around. Keep this relationship in mind. Stay in control of your body, otherwise it will be forced to try and gain control of itself. It doesn't want to do this, but someone has to be in charge. The body isn't really designed for this, and might get damaged in the process. Please remember, you are the one in charge, you are the one who's responsible for what happens to your body. Without your body, returning *Home* will be physically impossible for you.

Okay, okay, things are getting a little on the serious side. i wouldn't want to end this part of our discussion with another lecture, so let's have a little fun with your imagination. During the time that we've been together, i've been watching as your mind played with various possibilities on how i might look. i have to say, i'm very flattered with some of these pictures of me. You've been very kind and quite creative.

Since *the Gathering* came together, we've been using other ways to recognize each other. We don't need to rely on our 'looks' anymore. Truth is, i haven't thought much about how i used to look before then. I know that you like having an image to work with, when it comes to thinking about certain people in your life. And, since i'm definitely a part of your life now, i've decided to give you a little hint about how i really look. i am not a man, nor am i a woman. i am a bit of both. i have male and female qualities, but i've never actually been a person. Use your imagination, as we get to know each other, and if one picture seems to be popping-up again and again, then i'll become that person for you.

Chapter 22

Your Body is Asleep

Welcome - i'm Una. As you enter this next phase of the presentation, you will notice that your previous impressions of the world have changed. This is due to the fact that *The Body Sensual* is now asleep. While it sleeps, most of its senses are placed on "standby." This is a normal part of living in the world and one that has many advantages, as you shall soon see.

One of the first things you'll notice is that while your body sleeps, you remain very much awake. Isn't it strange how just a few moments ago, you were feeling so tired. And, now this feeling has gone. *The Body Sensual* does need its rest, however you do not. *Reality* knows this fact and has designed a special section where you may continue to enjoy yourself during these "off" times.

When you visit this area, you'll soon discover that the normal rules of *Reality* no longer apply. You're able to do a lot more, without the limitations of the physical body holding you down. Unfortunately, many of our guests come here thinking they are still in their bodies. As a result, they miss-out on many of our unique attractions. Lucky for them, it doesn't take too long to realize that something is definitely different about this place. They can fly, move through time and they're meeting all kinds of strange, new friends. While these unusual events help to bring them to the possibilities of this wonderful space, it doesn't complete the process.

This final key to the magic of the *Dreaming* is a long and gradual training of the person's mind. It brings them to a point where they're able to concentrate on what they're doing while they're here, and remember what happened when they awaken into their body. Interacting within this area is so different from the physical world, that the process of getting used to it needs time. You might forget which is the world and which is the *Dreaming*. Have you ever returned to your body after a night in the *Dreaming*, and for just a moment thought you were still there? This is the kind of carryover effect we want to make sure doesn't happen. We want you to be sure of who and what you are, so you don't try flying while you're in your body, for instance. As you'll soon see, the *Dreaming* has many advantages to offer.

As you learn to use the *Dreaming* in the way that it was designed, your waking reality will soon become a lot more enjoyable for you. The Dreaming is an important source of knowledge for you and the others. It can help you understand why certain things seem to be happening in your world, and how to best deal with them. Think of it as a play area, where you can try different things, without their having any effect on your waking life. As you enter this area, think of something you would like to try, somewhere you would like to go, or someone with whom you would like to speak. These are only three of the possible choices. Now, these people, places or things don't necessarily have to exist in your waking reality. They could be imaginary. The point is, to try new things while you're here. There's nothing to fear.

The *Dreaming* is directly connected to your waking world. If you wanted to visit somewhere or someone, you could do so. Unfortunately, you could only do so as an observer. You could watch what was happening, but you couldn't actually do much in the way of taking part in what was happening, no matter how badly you wanted. The main reason for this problem lies in the simple fact that you have no body with which to interact. But, knowing what was happening, and then later remembering what happened, could help you when you returned to the waking world. Once you returned to the body, you could then do something about what you saw.

Many times, you will find that you are automatically sent to certain areas within the *Dreaming* and of *Reality*, itself. This is done with a purpose. When you realize you're in a new place, look at your surroundings. Are they familiar? Is there anyone you know, nearby? Now, think of why you might be in this particular place. Why would you have chosen to be here, or why would someone else want you there? When you feel like you have some idea; if possible, begin interacting with your surroundings and with the others who share this space. Do so with the purpose of finding important information. Your being there is not by accident! You have something to learn from this place, and from the others. There are many hints and clues all around you; helpful solutions which you can bring with you into the waking world and which can be used to make your life more enjoyable. Feel free to make good use of this unusual opportunity.

One of the basic rules behind the *Dreaming*, is the idea of "like attracts like." When your body moves into sleep, you will naturally go to areas and attract other guests according to how you're feeling and what you're thinking. The result is always a combination of your thoughts and feelings. So, no matter how hard you try to think yourself somewhere, it won't work if your feelings are needing something else. If you're feeling angry or sad as you fall asleep, and your thoughts are filled with images that relate to these feelings, then you will likely go to areas where others are experiencing the same thing. In this way, you can all work together to help one another, or to find a common solution. Often, this is actually the case. You're all there working on the same problem, be it in the modern era or within some historic or future time period. It doesn't actually matter, you see, for the problems of our guests carry over from time period to time period. Just because it's the future doesn't mean that personal problems have changed. Things don't actually get better; we just change the way in which the problem presents itself. For example, poverty and violence are the same in any era.

Without the limits of time and space, you're now free to explore any when and any where you like! As well, you can enjoy what's called *Power Sessions* while your body rests. These "naps" let you explore the *Dreaming* in a way that feels as though you've been away for a long time, when it was really just a few brief moments in time. Using this facility works best when your body is neither too tired, nor very alert. As you may already know, some of your most memorable sessions occur just before you return to the body. These are the ones we especially want you to remember, and bring back into the waking world with you.

Though this dream world may seem disorganized and full of surprises, it's actually very well designed. It's equipped with hidden safety features. For instance, you may not realize this, but each of you has a unique identifier. This little tag allows us to keep track of where you are and what you're doing. It may seem like we're spying, but it would be more accurate to think of us as watching over you. We simply want to be ready, in case you need our help. We want to assure you that you're safe and sound. Actually, the Identifier tool isn't simply for our use, it can be used by anyone. It's a great way to find someone and, once again, you're not limited by time or space. All you need to do is want to be with them, and you're there. The only drawback is, they might not recognize you when you find them. You see, the *Dreaming* is a very personal space. Each of you experiences this area in your own way. If you're planning to visit with someone, let him or her know ahead of time, so they can expect you. It'll make things much easier.

Think of your time here as a vacation from your everyday life. The *Dreaming* allows you the freedom to explore anything you wish, and with anyone you choose. It really is a chance to dream and to imagine the impossible. Just think of it.

i hope this brief presentation has been helpful in some way, and i look forward to seeing you upon one of your many visits to our new facility. Enjoy!

Chapter 23

Bax here.

Most of what Una said is fairly helpful, but there are a few things she didn't say about the *Dreaming*. Because it's so limitless, this area of *Reality* can be a lot of help in getting you *Home*. Though she's well aware of this fact, Una would rather you didn't know this. It's her job to make sure you're happy when you visit. She doesn't want you to suddenly decide that you've had enough. She wants you to stay as long as possible.

The *Dreaming* is a great source of information for everyone. It contains all of the experiences of everyone who has ever visited, and will ever visit *Reality*. And, that includes you! It has 'short-cuts" and pieces of advice for the trip *Home* that you just won't find anywhere else. In the same way that Una was inviting you to really make use of your dreaming to have more fun, i'm going to encourage you to learn how to understand the language of your dreams.

Do you remember when we were talking about how your memory works? It stores your memories as pictures and objects. The dream world does a similar thing. When you're looking for answers there you will need to see things in a new way, a way that's different from when your body is awake. You will need to see everything in your dreams as standing for something else, or representing something.

Everything in the *Dreaming* has a meaning, just like all of those things stored in your memory. In your dreams, the meaning is hidden inside everything you see. How can you unlock these hidden secrets? You just ask! It takes some practice a first, but that's basically the secret to finding the information.

The first mistake is in not realizing that you're dreaming.

With some practice, and a feeling of really wanting to be successful, you will realize one night that you're dreaming. And, while still in the dream, you will ask someone "What's the meaning of this dream?". They will tell you; they *have* to tell you. The answer will be simple. Remember it.

Chapter 24

Speaking of learning languages, i'd like to take you back to a time before you were born. Yes, it's possible for you to remember that far back, if you want to. And, yes, you were alive before your birthday.

Before you were brought into this lifetime, you had the ability to communicate. You had a unique way of expressing your thoughts and emotions to the others. This original language, or "mother tongue" if you like, is very different from the way you try to express your ideas now. Your new language, the one you're now using to read these pages, is a "second-hand" sort of language. It's good, but it's not as good as the original. When you use your original way of communicating, there are no mix-ups or misunderstandings. Everything is clear and obvious to the one with whom you're in conversation. Actually, there's no real sense of a conversation, because the whole idea is sent all-at-once. It's complete, much like a picture. You don't ever need to explain yourself. All the humor, all the emotion is packaged together in one single thought. Because there's no sense of time involved, you have their side of the conversation as well. It's very efficient, but you may find it a little boring, preferring a long casual conversation with your friends or the mysterious, carefully chosen interplay of words with that attractive stranger.

It's not that your original language was taken away from you when you came here. Rather, you decided that no one was getting the messages you were sending, and so you decided to learn the language they were using, so that you could get things like food and attention. You were a very smart baby, you know. As time went on, you tried again and again to use the original language but no one was listening. The secondary language was going to have to do, if you were to make any sense out of this new world. As i've said, this new language is good, and can come very close to the original through things like poetry, literature and theatre, but there's still the issue of time and interpretation by the one who's receiving it. Like your body said, everyone has their own personal way of seeing things in the world, even if this thing is shown to many people in the exact, same way. These very words, though they are printed over and over as the same sentences, making the same book, will generate many different combinations of feelings and thoughts for the many readers it will eventually reach. That's why we're trying to use very simple language. We don't want there to be any misunderstandings with our readers. Try as we might, there are bound to be a few opinions on what we're really saying to you. Let me just remind you, there is nothing between the lines; just space.

As you've probably guessed by now, your original tongue is much like the language of your dreaming and your memory. It would make perfect sense, wouldn't it? After all, you were able to remember and to dream from the day you were born. Do you see the connection? By working to learn even one of these languages, you'll be mastering all three, and there's more. Through this learning process, you will actually improve in your relationships with others.

Have you ever felt misunderstood?

You'll begin to really understand what they're trying to say to you, many times before the words ever fully come out. With practice, you'll read their messages as little mental images. You won't actually be listening 'word for word' anymore. Instead, you'll be getting an impression about them. Isn't this better? Isn't this always what you had hoped to be able to do? It's communicating without all the 'mind-reading.'

You're all really good at sending messages; that's not the problem. Receiving them and reading them more clearly, will help to bring communicating back into balance for everyone. It's a natural process; you can't turn it off while you're there. No matter what you do, your thoughts and feelings are constantly being sent away for everyone to read. These messages are swirling all around you. All you need to do is remember how to open them. Once enough of you start doing this, you'll start to see the return of something called *Word*. This isn't actually its real name, but this is as close as i can get to describing it.

Word is a state of mind; it's a certain way of thinking about the world. It's the next big step for all of you. i can tell you that it's coming, but i'm not allowed to say when. There are a lot of you who are learning to use your original language now, and a few others who are really good at using it. But, for *Word* to come back, there has to be a certain number of you who actually get it, while living in the same time period. That's been the tricky part over the years. What usually happens is that many of you don't realize this until you're older, and then, just as everyone is ready to welcome it back, a few of you go through the death event and it gets put-off for a while. It's better for you and the others to learn it while you're younger. Thankfully, you only need to be in the same time period, and not the same location! Your world is getting closer to that 'magic number' again, and we're doing all we can to help you reach it.

Even though I can't tell you when it will happen, I can give you some hints about what will happen when you do reach "critical mass." On that day, everyone will go through the experience, no one will be left out. Now, even though i just said you'll all experience it, that doesn't mean you'll be receiving it in exactly the same way. It's personal. You all look very different from one another, even though you're essentially, the same. Those little differences are what make the experience unique. But, it's the common or shared part that allows all of you to receive the experience at the same time. It's the important part, the one that brings you closer to *Home*.

When it happens, the laws of *Reality* that have to do with time and space will be replaced with something new. 'Day/night', 'near/far', 'us/them', as well as many other Earth-based concepts, will all change. They'll need to, in order to make room for *Word*. You'll learn more about this in *Article 4*.

Getting back to the subject of dreaming, i need to tell you that what happens in your dreams is not *Reality*. It's the *Dreaming*. They're related, but different. Many of you would like to believe that your dreams might come true, that they are messages of what's coming. Believing that your dreams will come true, whether these were good dreams or bad, sets you into a trap. This belief will always lead to unhappiness, either because the good dream didn't come true, or because the bad one *did*. At this time, it's best if you think of your dreams as being just dreams. They happened in another, very different place from the one you're in when your body is awake. Your dreams can still be valuable and special, just the way they are. Think of them as helpful, or not-so-helpful experiences. These experiences are now over, but can still be remembered when you need them.

The *Dreaming* has its own rules, just as the waking world does. It's important to respect the differences between the two. Maybe one day you won't have to respect these differences, but for now, it's best to think of them as unique in their own way. Listen carefully; the borders separating the *Dreaming* and the waking worlds are beginning to fall apart. It's a gradual process, so there's no need to worry. Everything changes in your world. The dissolving of these borders is no different. This is part of the reason we're hoping you'll spend some time getting to appreciate the differences between the two worlds of waking and sleeping. As the process gets farther along, there will be times when you're not quite sure if you're awake or asleep. It might get confusing for you. If you've gotten to know these two worlds well enough, these strange times won't bother you. You'll just switch your thinking according to where you find yourself. Your ability to do this will be extremely important when *Word* returns to *Reality*. The others may need your help in adjusting to the change. Just as well, you'll be needing their help too. Everyone will have their part to play, and it will be a great success!

My final advice to you is simple.

Sleep well my friend, and Dream!

Chapter 25

Your Personality

Being and acting human isn't only about having fun in the physical world. There are many other parts of you that need to be explored. When we say the word 'personality', we are really talking about all of those 'bits and pieces' that came to you while you were learning. From the day you arrived, you've been discovering everything you could about your world, and the others who share it with you. You've learned a lot, and if you add it all up, that learning comes out as your personality, the way you act. You don't always act the same way. We know this. Different friends and events will lead you to all kinds of actions and re-actions. You will act one way in front of someone you like, and another way with others who seem strange to you. Either way, you're acting. If you think about it, you've learned so many ways of acting, and all of them are ready for you now, right when you need them.

For some reason, i feel like you might be in the mood for a story, so i'm going to tell you one about a little snowball. It's not a very exciting story, but i think it's pretty good for my first time at doing something like this. (It's not that much fun telling stories in *The Gathering*. Everyone already knows the ending.)

The Snowball

A tiny, little snowball was born one evening, on top of a very high mountain. It was very special in its own way, even if it was so very small. At first, no one much noticed it, being so tiny and so high up. But after a little while and with help of a few passing snowfalls, it began to grow. Each little snowflake that happened upon it, stuck to it and made a special connection with the tiny snowball. With time, this little snowball grew large enough to gather some weight of its own. It didn't feel so little anymore.

Growing in size meant that the snowball could see more and more of its world. The snowball liked this, and thought it might be nice to learn about new places. But, how could the snowball do this? It decided to wait and see what might happen. Then, one windy night, as the snowball was worrying over the idea that it had grown a bit lopsided in its shape, something happened. It rolled over. This was a big surprise to the snowball, who had never really moved much before. It was a bit scary, actually. Then it happened again, and again! It rolled a little bit to the left and then to the right, each time picking-up speed, with a lot of help from the wind. With the added speed came added snowflakes, sticking here and there, around its cool, sparkling body. 'What's happening?', thought the snowball. Things we're changing very quickly. 'i don't know if i like this anymore, but how do i make it stop?'

The snowball was becoming much easier to see, from below the mountaintop, but no one bothered to look up. No one ever noticed what was happening. Moving faster and faster, racing down the mountainside, it began picking up bits of rock, small twigs and many other little items, along the way. It looked like a very different snowball now. Realizing this, the snowball thought it would change its name to Snow-boulder. Snow-boulder was used to the traveling and growing now, it wasn't as afraid, anymore.

As time passed, Snow-boulder grew so large that moving became difficult for it. It began slowing down. But this didn't really bother Snow-boulder, who was very happy to have grown so large and to have seen so many things while traveling. That was, until one-day Snow-boulder stopped completely.

Snow-boulder was in quite a spot, having grown so big and heavy with snow and all of the other things it picked-up, along the way. Being in a place lower on the mountainside also meant that the weather was a bit warmer now. Things seemed different here. What would it do? What *could* it do? Just like before, Snow-boulder decided to wait. It waited, and it waited.

While it was waiting, a strange thing happened. Someone looked up, and saw Snow-boulder. This certain someone felt amazed about what they saw, and wanted a closer look. She gathered a few friends together, and they also gathered a few more friends, and all of them began to climb the mountain. Before long they reached Snow-boulder, who was still waiting and unfortunately, melting.

The people could see that Snow-boulder was melting, and wondered that they should do something about this. They talked awhile and eventually came to a decision. They were going to roll Snow-boulder back up the mountain where the temperature was cooler. This way, Snow-boulder would last much longer and the people would always be able to look up and enjoy seeing Snow-boulder. But there was a problem; Snow-boulder was too big and too heavy to move by themselves. Somehow, they would need to make Snow-boulder smaller and lighter.

This would be easy for them to do, but they would need to begin right away. They removed all of the extra snow and rock and branches and leaves from Snow-boulder. They smoothed the rough and bumpy surfaces and didn't stop working until Snow-boulder was ready for moving. As you can imagine, Snow-boulder was very surprised with all that was happening. As bit by bit was taken from its surface, Snow-boulder could see that so much of what was being removed really wasn't necessary for its survival. It was all just a lot of extra stuff. Getting rid of it actually felt good. Soon, Snow-boulder began to feel itself moving. It was headed back towards its original home, higher up the mountainside.

They pushed and pushed, with all the strength they had, until after some time, they found just the right place for Snow-boulder. The temperature was just right here, and from below, the people would always be able to look up and see it. As it turned-out, the people really needed Snow-boulder to be here. They needed a reason to look up, away from their daily problems and challenges. And, for many, there was a needed sense of comfort in knowing that something was watching over them.

Snow-boulder lived this way for a long, long time. But all things eventually pass in this world, and the people decided that other things were more important. They eventually looked beyond Snow-boulder, but never forgot that it had once been there, and what the people did that special day.

*

In many ways, your personality is just like Snow-boulder. You add so many bits and pieces to your personality, from everything and everyone with whom you come into contact. It makes this lifetime seem so rich and exciting for you! There is one point in the story that i would like to focus on, however. It's the part where Snow-boulder slows down and eventually stops. We'll call this *The Turning Point*.

At this stage, Snow-boulder might feel as if things are finished and done. It feels happy and satisfied with everything that's happened in its lifetime. But, just because you're happy and feeling complete, doesn't mean you're finished.

Feeling satisfied isn't the goal.

The Turning Point is the place you come to when, for one reason or another, your lifetime seems to have stopped moving. It feels like nothing much is happening; nothing's really changing for you. i'm sure you've experienced moments like these. Most of the time, these turning points feel quite satisfying and restful; like you've achieved something, or come to a nice, comfortable place in your life. But, after a while, these feelings start to fade and you begin to do some serious wondering. Are you really satisfied? Is this the place you really wanted to be, or is there something more? In a similar way, this is what's happened to our friend the Snow-boulder. It has come to a place in its brief lifetime, where it is now forced to make some decisions about what to do next. *The Turning Point* offers you the chance to do this.

In some ways this can be forced upon you. Like the Snow-boulder, you will reach a point where you've taken something as far as it needs to go. Whether it's a job, a relationship, or even where you're living, all these parts of your lifetime will eventually reach *The Turning Point*. When they do, you've come to the end of something and now it's time to think about moving in a new direction. These events are all part of your personality's development. Each one builds and shapes the personality you play, as well as the person you will eventually become. Every stage forms a piece of the puzzle that is your lifetime. You are learning. Your personality is learning and growing.

As the story shows us, help is always available at *The Turning Point*. Growing and learning as a person within *Reality*, means changing in some way. If we think about Snow-boulder, it's going to have to change if it wants to get rolling again. As a person moves through different stages in their lifetime, they will find that they have to make changes, if their personality is to grow. If they want to become a certain kind of person, or play a certain role, then they will have to adjust their personality to fit with the new role they want to play.

Some things will stay and others will need to go. But happily, something new will also be added. i know you like new things. Most of the changes and adjustments will only take place on the surface of your personality, anyway. Like the original 'snowball' part of the Snow-boulder, the inner part of your personality will always stay with you. This is the part that was made during the beginning stages of your development, or what you call your 'childhood.'

Your personality is the role you play.

You can't 'have it all', as far as your personality goes. If you want to play a certain role in this lifetime, you'll want to make some changes to your personality, to fit with that new role. There are parts of you now that won't fit with that new picture of yourself, so they'll eventually have to go. You will either let them go, or they will be taken from you. It was your choice. Trust me when i say that it's easier to let them go. Letting them go allows you to trade them for something new. Trading is usually an enjoyable experience for you. On the other hand, when something is taken by force, it usually causes you pain. Pain is something you don't enjoy. i won't say anymore about this right now. You've obviously got the picture.

There is another part of growing that's important to think about. Sometimes being able to control the process won't matter all that much to you. At first, the snowball did some of the changing on purpose, or as we like to say in *The Gathering, with* purpose. This is important for getting things started. But after things got rolling in the direction it wanted, it just let the rest of the changes happen on their own. It rolled along and occasionally bumped into this and knocked into that, each time shaping and building itself into something new. These little adjustments are still important to the process, but they don't need as much energy as those first few steps. The snowball was already going to where it wanted; it just needed small nudges to keep it on track. Your human growing process is the same.

Enjoying your time here, on this tiny planet, can only be done in accepting that you will change. It's one of those "facts of life". As well, everyone and everything else will also change. No one will ever stay the same, no matter how much you want them to. The best that you can do is to let these changes come and to welcome them when they do. They are always for the better and, one way or another, they will always lead you *Home*.

Chapter 26

In the same way that the Earth experiences it's four seasons, your person can also show itself to the world in four main ways. If you want, you can think of these four ways as moving from the stages of 'birth' to 'death.' While they generally look like the four seasons you're about to meet, they aren't quite the same. You see, while the four seasons tell you about a gradual movement from being young to growing old, i will be talking about how these four are always with you now, in every moment. They're with you all the time, no matter how things might look on the outside. Sadly, you aren't able to show these four at the same time, because they need to take turns, but they're with you just the same. This means that it's possible for a very small child to act very wise and mature, and a very old person to act like a child.

Knowing about these four, personal seasons is important for getting you through your daily life. No matter what you're doing, you'll always be using one of them. You'll always act in one of four, basic ways. This might sound a bit simple, but that's because there's a big range of ways for acting within each one. Lots of people will try to tell you that one of these ways is better than the others, but each is very useful in reaching your goals. Learning about them, and knowing which one best fits the moment, can really help you. The four seasons are equally important; no season is better than the other. As i said earlier, when we talked about *The Body Sensual* and the *Dreaming*, the four seasons you're about to meet aren't actual people. They're ways that a person can act. But, you can also use them as 'extras' to strengthen whatever role you'd like to play. The seasons can make you more convincing, when you're acting. Just like before, they will be speaking through me and the information will be about *Reality*, not your actual *Home*.

As you read through this information, ideas and images will appear in your mind. You'll start to imagine new things. Some of these will seem "good" to you, and others will look "strange." They're all just pictures in your mind, and these pictures will come and go. They need to, if you're going to really understand the information. Sorting and organizing pictures is how the brain learns new things. It compares the new things to ones it already knows. Let the brain do its job, and enjoy the show!
Let's begin…

winter
i am the idea of everything that exists, before it is born. i am like a seed, hidden below the surface of all that you see. i always wait for just the right moment, before i show myself. i am what could be, and what *will* be. Once i appear, everything changes.

In choosing to live a human lifetime in *Reality*, many plans were made. i hold all these plans for you. Even though you've forgotten about them, they're still here with me. Your plans are safe.

Because you forget about your plans when you're born into *Reality*, I am able to help you by connecting with you, through your imagination. This helps you to remember small pieces of your plans, and then build on them. This arrangement works well in your case, but many other people seem to be having difficulty with it. They are distracted from using their imaginations, and miss many chances to connect with me. And so, i wait.

I know your plans. Because of this, i can tell you about the future. i see your lifetime, all at once. I don't wait for time and i don't need a place. You might say that i carry many secrets, but they're only secrets you've forgotten.

You might know me by another name, i am also the *Unexpected*...

Bax here. Like winter, i can also see that the future has already happened. I can tell you that it was a big surprise to winter when you decided to use your imagination to form a new plan for the future, a plan that was different from the ones it knew. Let me show this to you in another way. As we said to you near the beginning of this book, when you chose your program for this lifetime, you included all the events that would happen. That's where winter comes in. It has a copy of this program and thinks you'll follow it. What it doesn't know is that you're able to make some changes to your program, and that you've actually done this.

Your future is both pre-planned and changeable.

If you go along with what your lifetime offers you, then you're pretty much following your program. But if you're fighting against some of what your lifetime offers, then you're choosing to move away from the future that was planned for you. In other words, you're resisting fate. Sometimes this can help and sometimes this can hurt. But the choice is always yours. We'll talk more about this later.

As far as using winter in the way you act, you are most like winter during those times when you are waiting patiently for things to change. You're not in any hurry because you feel like something or someone will come at just the right time, and then things will begin to change again.

spring

i am the beginning of everything that happens during your lifetime and the growing stage of your plans and ideas. I make everything seem new and exciting for you. When I arrive, you feel the urge to start your plans within *Reality*. winter is the source of who i am, and lives before me. i don't really have any ideas or plans of my own, i just help you get things done. i will wake you in the morning, and keep you focused until you're finished. If you ever feel that i'm not around, it's because you don't actually need my help anymore.

One of the things you'll be doing in *Reality* is growing a human body. This will take some time, but i'll be with you.

Because you'll be new to the idea of time, you'll feel that growing your body is either taking too long, or moving too quickly. The growing will involve changes, lots of changes, but you'll be happy when you're complete. Happiness is the way you will feel when your plans are done. It's a good experience within *Reality*. When an experience is not good within *Reality*, you'll call it bad. If your plans are taking too long to finish, or aren't getting done, you will feel unhappy. We don't want you to feel unhappy while you're in *Reality*, so i'll be sure to always be there to help you with your plans.

Bax here. spring touched on some good points, and will be very helpful in getting you *Home*. spring not only helps you with the plans of your original *Reality* program, they help you with *all* of your plans! spring doesn't care which plans, just as long as they're helping you.

spring also talked about feelings. Feelings are something you know a lot about. We won't even try to tell you about your personal feelings, at this point. This is because you actually know more about them than we do. We don't really know much about the human feelings; they seem strange to us. The information we have, seems to say that these feelings are somehow connected with *The Body Sensual*. There is a connection between your feelings and living in a human body. The two seem to depend on each other. Our existence is different from yours, and since we have never had a human body, we will not pretend to know something we do not. If we did, you would realize this very quickly and it would ruin any trust you have allowed during our communication together. Our connection would fade. From what we can see, human feelings affect the way people act. Some of you try to hide your feelings at times. This is just another way of acting, really.

summer

You are complete in some way, perhaps many things are complete, when i arrive. spring has gone.

i will stay with you now, in this peaceful state.

The Gathering here. With summer, challenges and the *Unexpected* arrive, but you feel capable in facing them. You now have the ability to respond to them, an ability you call 'responsibility.' Choices always need to be made. The time to make these choices is always now. With summer, the answers suddenly seem simple and clear. Another important thing you realize is that the results of these choices naturally take on a life of their own. In other words, you won't be able to control them anymore. This won't bother you.

These moments of summer won't last long. *Reality* likes to keep things moving and changing, for your entertainment. Knowing this, and knowing that summer will return again and again, all you need to do when summer *does* arrive is notice the difference in the way you are acting. This is important.

Out of the four, summer is the season most like the experience of being *Home*. When we mentioned noticing certain things, it was because remembering them will help you find *Home*. If you notice them, you will remember them. In summer, you are acting like your Self. During the other seasons, you will often act like the others. Acting like the others, is not the best way of getting *Home*.

autumn
i am the 'letting-go' of all things, from *Reality*. As you begin to experience completion during your visit, you'll start to let go of certain things. You won't need them anymore. Some of these things will leave on their own. As for the rest, the others will help you get rid of them. In the same way, when you come to the end of your program within *Reality*, a stage called 'fullness,' you will let go of much more. All that you see of *Reality* must be left behind, for the others. *Reality* is self-contained and because of this, nothing is ever lost. Everything is used again.

The Gathering here. autumn can be the most difficult experience of the four. Be aware of its purpose. In order for *Reality* to function properly, it needs you and the others to let go. The fact that so many of you are 'holding on' to things and persons, actually makes going *Home* more difficult for you. Everyone is getting attached or 'sticking' to things and getting stuck. autumn can't do its job, because of this. Normally, we might be advising you and the others to act against the workings and goals of *Reality*, but this situation is different. We can't get *Home* if we are stuck.

autumn sends a bit of a warning to you. Whenever you refuse to let go of something, it will eventually be taken from you. The reason this happens, is because it's needed somewhere or some when else in *Reality*. If something is taken before you are finished with it, the experience of completion goes missing for you. This experience is one of the main reasons why you keep coming back, again and again. You are trying to 'complete' your experience, relative to the thing that was taken. The solution to this is simple.

Pretend it's not really yours to keep.

Think of the things within *Reality* as belonging to *Reality*. You are just borrowing them or using them, while you are visiting. That way, it's much easier to let them go, and you won't get stuck.

Probably the biggest act of letting-go happens in relation to your person, or who you believe you are, as you come to the end of your stay in *Reality*. Many of you don't want to lose yourself. You won't. You are not your person, so you can't possibly lose your Self. Your person doesn't belong to you, it belongs to *Reality*. You were simply borrowing it as part of the *Reality* experience. The 'death' of this person should not be thought of as your own end.

There is no 'Life and Death'....... only Life.

One thing you don't have to leave in *Reality* is the memory of your visit. You will leave with a complete and detailed memory of your experience. The memory will be whole, and yours to keep.

The four seasons have been shown to you as separate, but they only look that way because of the way you see and understand things through your experience of time and place. They will begin to appear differently for you in the coming weeks and months. Instead of looking like stages in your human lifetime, or patterns in the weather of your planet, the idea of their being with you in every moment will start to grow. They will start to be ways of acting and responding, as you move through your day. You'll see them coming and going at just the right moments, to help you with all of the constant changes that *Reality* has provided for your enjoyment. Does this make good sense to you?

As well, making good use of these four will help connect you with memory on a deeper level, causing you to ask questions about the past. Answering those questions, in time, will let you know if and in what ways, you may be 'stuck.' Even as we mention this point, your memory is quickly looking at the possibilities. Be patient with yourself and with the process. There is no need to hurry.

Chapter 27

As we come to the close of this article's discussion, we see that our line of communication has maintained itself quite well. It has also changed in some ways. Your need of a more personal, 'friendly' style of messaging doesn't seem to be of any real importance to you, now that you know us a little better. Even so, we will do our best to imitate the style used by Bax, to further strengthen our connection with you. This change is a helpful one, particularly as your friend Bax is no longer available to you, in this way. Bax has entered *Reality*.

This was a free choice; there was no accident or mistake that led to Bax joining you in *Reality*. It was agreed that Bax might be better able to assist you and the others by being present with you, as you journey *Home*. It is often seen in your world that changes can be better achieved from 'within the system.' A specific program and role was selected to enable Bax to achieve this, one that hasn't been chosen in a very long time.

Know that Bax is with you in a new way, and that you are now being helped from within and from without.

Initiating *Article three*...

Article Three - The Others

Chapter 28

You are not alone within *Reality*. There are many others with you. Do you know who they are?

The Unfolding Drama

The others are characters, and they have names. You will come to know them in a personal sense. You may like them, or you may not; your feelings about them won't really matter. Your thoughts about them *will* matter, however. As far as this Article is concerned, the others only ask that you meet with them and get to know them. This is for the sake of your journey *Home*. They know what you are trying to do because they are attempting the very same thing. They are real. They will be as brief as possible in what they say and they can be trusted. They want you to be successful.

Before you meet with them, we want to say a few things. First, the big idea supporting this Article is one that is already known to you. You are an actor. Everything else will revolve around this.

Secondly, you will be inter-acting with the others. They are actors, too. One difference between you and the others is, they may not know they are acting. It's not your role to tell them that they are acting; it's ours. At times, you too will forget you're acting. This is part of the process. It's easy to get distracted within *Reality*. We will do all we can to help you, until you reach *The Reference Point*. After that, you won't need us to remind you. Things and events will seem clear.

Getting ready for your performance

There is an important reason why your lifetime has placed you in this time and place. You're here to complete your program, just like everyone else. You must pay off old debts and leave with a clean slate. (unless you have chosen to use the loophole from *Article two*.)

In this way, *Reality* is actually helping you, though it doesn't realize it. Make the most of this opportunity. You're in the right place, at the right time, to achieve your short and long-term goals. Knowing this, the present moment becomes extremely valuable. The others become valuable, too! Obviously, they are valuable of themselves, because they are real. But, they are also valuable in their interactions. Your interactions are mutually beneficial.

Just like in the dreaming worlds, you will be drawn to people and places that are acting and feeling in a similar way to how you are thinking and feeling in the moment, or in general. Manage your own thoughts and feelings; don't let them take control of you. This will allow you to indirectly select your co-actors as well as the conditions for your performance. Another benefit lies in the obvious condition of never having to face your challenges alone. There will always be others there to share in the experience with you.

Choose to be *here*.
Stop wishing you were somewhere else.

Set

The strangest thing about location within *Reality,* is how humans imagine it. All of your performances will happen somewhere. They happen within *Reality.* No matter where or when you appear to be, we would like you to simply think of it all as one thing, *Reality.*

Many of you are dazzled by the many different locations and time periods that present themselves to you, when choosing your *Reality* programs. There really seems to be no end to the possibilities! But, from where we see things, all the locations are the same. They just wear a different appearance for you.

Let's think of it this way. A theatre presents many different plays over the course of a season. All of the plays are performed on the same stage. The only thing that changes are the sets. ***Reality* is the stage.** The stage is always the same, no matter what decorations are placed upon it. When you imagine a play, think about the stage that sits behind all of the drama. It holds everything up, and supports all of the performances. Imagine looking 'through' the sets, the props, the actors to what's actually there, in a more permanent sense. We want you to see past all the temporary things, to the ones that are always there. Can you do this? Let's give it a try...

Look around you now. Begin to separate everything gradually. First point out the things that will change in the next few moments, the actions, the weather, the sounds, etc. Now move on to the things that will change by tomorrow, and so on. When you reach the end of this exercise, you may find yourself in a strange position. Is anything you see actually permanent? Nothing seems to last, for some reason. When you get to this point in the exercise, you're ready to see *Reality*. At this point, all you need to be, is ready.

Props

Everything in *Reality* has a purpose, and that purpose is to get you *Home*. But you need to use these things in the right ways. Look around you now. Do all of the objects in your view have a purpose? If they don't seem to have a purpose for you, perhaps they might be more useful to someone else. Not everything has been put here for your own, personal benefit. Others need help, too.

All that you have; all your money and possessions should be thought of in a new way. They are all tools to support the goal of returning. When you think of them in this way, they become priceless. What could be more important? Your time here is temporary and everything in *Reality* stays in *Reality*, so the goal is to use the props, not keep them. Props are here to support the actors and their actions. The actors know that once the scene is over, the props can be put aside. There's no need to keep holding-on to them.

Wardrobe

Clothing is important, both in the care of *The Body Sensual* and for the roles you are playing. Clothing and Props are similar in many ways. One important difference between the two is the effect they have on your acting abilities. Clothing, makeup, and hair design have a much stronger effect upon these abilities. They can make you a better actor, from the point of view of your co-actors and surrounding audience.

Being a better actor inspires others in their roles.

Chapter 29

Direction

Your interactions improve when each of you appears more convincing in your separate roles. One way you can be more convincing is to know that you're acting, *while* you're acting. This allows you to be more aware of what you're doing and saying, so that you can make any needed improvements to your performance, while the other person interacts with you.

You have everything you need to play any role you like, but there are some parts you weren't meant to play in this lifetime. Those roles were given to others. Sorry to disappoint you, but aren't you also relieved at the same time? Doesn't this take away some of the responsibility you might have been feeling around having to be 'everything and everyone' to a special someone? It's unrealistic to expect it from yourself or anyone else. Each of you has selected a program with a certain number of roles and these are enough to get you *Home*. But how are you to know which ones are yours?

The clues or cues that will help you answer this question, can be connected to one simple word, 'appearances.' Think about the way you dress, the way you speak and behave. Do you tend to follow certain styles and avoid others? These styles are also connected with certain roles in your acting culture. Culture is about how we do everything, how we are living a lifetime. Think about the things you're good at, the things that seem easier for you.

Getting *Home* wasn't supposed to be that hard.

Sadly, one of the first things that happens when people realize they want to go *Home* while they're still in *Reality*, (and this is happening quite a lot in your time frame) is they decide they don't want to play their roles. They start to resist and rebel against *Reality*, which only keeps them there longer. The solution to this problem has already been given to you. You are an actor playing certain roles, who knows they're acting and who knows that playing these roles will get them *Home*.

Many people think there might be something false in this type of behavior, but *Reality itself* is false. You've come here to pretend haven't you? Then let's pretend for a moment, and you'll start to see the truth in what we're saying. Some of your happiest times as a child-human were when you were playing 'make-believe.' Even as a child, you knew you were pretending; you were acting and knew it was all an act. But, certain 'new' ideas have stolen this away from you. Pretending is nowadays seen as impractical. It doesn't serve a purpose. Today you're seeing it's true purpose.

As a little something extra, we'd like to say that playing your roles and knowing you're playing them, helps to shrink time. Yes, time is flexible! We'll speak more about this in a future Article.

Script

Knowing what to say, while you're acting, will involve connecting your memory with your ability to pretend. You'll soon see that the two of them go really well together. As a child, your pretending was a lot simpler because your Earth memories were only beginning. Now you have so much more with which to work. And, knowing about your memory from *Article two*, you won't have to worry about having to stop and think every time you want to say something. Your memory will quickly feed you the words as you speak them. (if you let it...) The pictures will arrive for you and release the needed dialogue, on cue.

Many of you like to feel more 'in control' of what you're saying, so the idea of using this more spontaneous kind of script might make you uncomfortable. Think about how much effort you use with your controlled way of speaking, how exhausting it might be. Relaxing into a new way of speaking will take some practice at first, but you'll soon see how it helps in making you a better actor.

Chapter 30

As *The Gathering*, we will now leave you in the presence of several, important characters. These are the others we told you about, at the start of chapter twenty-eight. They are characters, so they have the ability to appear in *Reality* when they are needed, and then disappear when they've finished their work. Humans can 'put on' or 'dress' in these characters whenever they want. Humans can then switch characters when a different kind of interaction presents itself. Do you understand? If you like, you can think of it as 'changing costumes.' The characters don't actually control the person, they just help with the acting. You might find that they resemble actual people, or certain types of people from your time period. This is no accident.

The Pretender

i welcome you and your efforts to return *Home*. i too am interested in returning. i call myself *The Pretender*, because i've become very good at acting in the way *The Gathering* has explained. i've also played *all* of the roles available within *Reality*, every, single one. i'm thankful that the number of roles was surprisingly limited. Don't worry, you won't need to do everything that i've done, in order to get *Home*. You're only responsible for the roles involved with your own program. Shall we continue?

i have complete access to *all* the available roles in *Reality*, but i'll only present you with the most beneficial ones. They'll be helpful both as roles that *you* can play, and as roles you'll be looking for in others, when you want to interact with them. In other words, *they* will be playing those other roles, not you. Showing you lots of unnecessary roles would be interesting, and give you plenty of information about them, but they would probably distract you from your wanting to get *Home*. After all, you didn't pick up this book to learn everything about *Reality*. The reason you picked it up was so you could get *Home*. Studying all of those other roles would probably make you want to return again and again, so you could actually play those roles. Yes, that's what happened to me...

One of the traps with acting is forgetting that you're acting. You'll know this is happening when you start to take things personally. It's okay to *act* like you're taking it personally, but you shouldn't really believe in it. When you do, you've forgotten who you are and why you're here. You've confused your real Self with the person you're pretending to be. You are not this character. You're much more, and quite different. If you're interested in the subject of believing, it will be shown to you in chapter 38.

When you take things personally, the acting stops and the reacting begins. Reacting involves doing things you've already done. Since you've already done them, they aren't much help to you. They don't count towards the process of getting you *Home*. Have you ever felt like reacting to things was a waste of time and energy, and that it really didn't get you anywhere? The kind of reacting i'm talking about is emotional. It's okay to have physical reactions to things. *The Body Sensual* needs to do this in order to keep itself functioning for you, and to reduce your experience of pain or discomfort.

The final thing i would like to remind you about is the idea of independent acting. There's no such thing in *Reality*. Everything you do and say affects the others in *Reality*, even when no one seems to be around. This is because everything and everyone is connecting to that 'stage' called *Reality*. Whether you're in the middle of an interaction or waiting your turn, you're still on the stage. Everyone is here and you're all together, so you are connected by it. But, you seem separate. Sometimes you might even seem isolated or distant. *Reality* is very convincing.

It's a good idea to depend on the others to play their part and to let the others know that they can depend on you. If someone seems to have forgotten their lines during the scene, just give them a moment. Don't try to rush them through it. Because of who you are, there's a very good chance that you'll already know their lines before *they* do. You have a knack for this. You can often see the whole scene unfolding, not simply your part in it. When this happens, try not to let the others know. They might not realize they're acting.

Chapter 31

Feelings

i am Orea. i'm going to share the results of my experiences with you. They will help you understand the importance of using feelings, as you perfect your acting skills.

As you've probably guessed, feelings are an amazing tool for convincing your audience of your superior skills in acting. i want you to be a great actor. i want to help you get *Home*.

Human feelings seem very real to you, and they can also be a source of strength in your world. When we're young, we are allowed to experience the full range of our feelings. This can be difficult for us at times, but it serves an important purpose. It builds emotional memories. As we grow older, we learn to manage our feelings so they don't take control of us. Eventually, as adults, we can draw from the source of our emotional memories when we need to, in order to achieve our acting goals. This *doesn't* mean that we won't continue to experience emotions. Our feelings are natural, at any age, and are part of the reason we've taken part in *Reality*.

As we start to grow in our acting abilities, the early stages of getting to know our feelings, without being controlled by them, can be thought of in this way:

> Feel sadness, do not *be* sad.
> Feel happiness, do not *be* happy.
> Feel anger, do not *be* angry.
> Feel joyful, and remember...

Because our feelings are exciting for us, we sometimes want to turn away from everything else, just to focus on them. If we focus on them too much, we start to let them take control. Noticing when this is happening will keep you from losing your way, from becoming lost in your feelings. Some of the interactions with the others will become very intense. A person can always bring intensity to their acting, without losing control.

One thing i'm noticing with humans is that you sometimes say you're feeling happy when you're really feeling angry or sad. There's a lot of social pressure on people nowadays to feel happy all the time. This is also an expectation we place upon ourselves. Just like many other things within *Reality*, we have some freedom to choose how we respond. My only recommendation is that if you say you're feeling happy, then *act* like it. Otherwise the others will notice that your words and acting don't match. In those moments you're not fooling anyone, not even yourself.

When we're really acting, we know we're not actually as sad, angry or happy as we might seem. At the time, we may not even be feeling *any* of these emotions. Thanks to our memory, we're able to look quickly to other times, so that we can act out those feelings as part of the show. We aren't acting out the old experiences, just the feelings from those experiences. *And*, we aren't feeling those feelings, just acting.

**We're using the past, in the present,
to improve the future.**

Up until this point in the book, it was good that you followed the message in the way it was presented to you. For the next few chapters, feel free to arrange the chapters in any way you like. Save the final chapter for the end, of course. As a final note, i would like to say that,

...the only thing you need to pay, is attention.

Initiating *the eight*....

Chapter 32

The Artist

i am Carri, one of the sisters. In earlier times, we were called by other names. We were present then, as now. We are related within *The Gathering,* and strive, always toward that event known as *The Revealing.* i'm here to remind you and the others that to imitate something or someone, delays the arrival of this event in some small way. *The Revealing* is important to you because it's the event that let's you know that the door is open for you to return *Home.* More will be said about this in *Article 4.*

In working toward this goal, i encourage you to imagine the *original.* The *original* exists as itself; there isn't a thing or person quite like it. Imagining it challenges you in an important way. It forces you to pay attention; it *startles* you. Nothing else affects you in quite the same way. If you gently search your memory, you'll find that some of the most important moments of your lifetime happened when you experienced a special something or someone for the very first time. *The original* changed you, and you haven't been the same since.

When you first experience something new and unusual, your common preoccupation with being distracted immediately stops and a clear moment arrives. The new item might appear as a work of art, a film, or song. We experience it in a way that says 'i want this.' That's the simplest way of saying it, and oftentimes you'll actually do whatever it takes to own the object. *The original* can't be owned. You already know this because after having the object with you for a while, you become bored with it. It doesn't give you the same experience any longer. It isn't original anymore. Then the search for something new starts all over again.

We sent *The original* into *Reality* to remind you of yourself. It gives you a momentary rest from all of the repetition. If you see it in this way, you'll know that you don't need to own an object or person, in order to appreciate them. You can enjoy them simply because they're there with you. If you still want to own the object, you can do so without expecting too much from it. Please remember that everything in *Reality* stays in *Reality*.

You are creative.

Even though you have an organized program to complete, you can still bring something new to the journey *Home*. Start with little things, unexpected things. Creativity often comes out of the *Unexpected*. You'll be doing something or speaking with someone, and your imagination will bring you a new option. It will say 'try this.' When this happens, you can trust that your imagination is helping you. It wouldn't risk taking you away from completing your program. These creative options are safe, and are designed to make your stay more enjoyable.

Your person was manufactured, actually. It's the only one of its kind. When certain others see your person, they recognize it as being special. They are drawn to it, and to you. When this happens, you'll know why. You startled them in a good way, and they'll never be the same again. It's what they were hoping, they just didn't realize it until now.

Chapter 33

The Psychic
i'm Alyia. There are many names that describe my purpose in *Reality*, but they all point to one thing, being able to see something you don't currently see. Many people come to me either hoping for answers, or to find agreement and support for something they already know. i didn't *sneak* into *Reality* in order to help you and the others. *Reality* actually *wants* me here. It wants me to help you with your program. When we're off track, our experience of *Reality* becomes painful for us. *Reality* does what it can, to prevent this from happening.

i can see your original program in certain ways and i can help you get back on track. My abilities to see your program can sometimes have limits. It's best if you have clear questions about what you need me to see. That helps me focus. Knowing a little about what you're going through can also give me a view that compares where you're at in your lifetime now, with where you had originally hoped to be.

> **There are plans made in the beginning,**
> **and plans we make along the way.**

Hopefully the two will match fairly closely. Because you forget all about those original plans when you arrive, the possibility for getting lost is very real. It happens a lot.

We sometimes find out early, that *Reality* does many things on purpose or, as i like to say, 'with purpose.' *Reality* will give you a little 'nudge' when you're headed away from your program, to let you know when you're making decisions that move you away from your plan. Sadly, we sometimes ignore these nudges. only paying attention to them when we have no other choice. By then, we could be pretty far off track. i remember you reading something in Chapter 29 about this. Being open to those little indicators can save you a lot of trouble. i realize how hard it is to stay focused on your plans, with all of the fun and excitement happening all around you. It's really all about perspective. Keeping your thoughts on your long-range goals can help you avoid those momentary opportunities that really don't get you anywhere.

Do you want 'fun' or *Home*?

Thinking about all i've just said, you may not actually need to visit with me all that often. Noticing that your lifetime is getting easier and more enjoyable, can provide you with the needed clues to see 'ahead' to the patterns connecting within your *own* program. In your world, specific choices naturally lead to certain results. It was planned this way. What are the results you're seeking?

There's a pace and a timing to your lifetime, that you also need to accept. We can't skip ahead, or rush to meet our goals, no matter how real they might seem. Every turn needs to be taken. When we try to rush things, we'll start missing those little nudges again, and get sidetracked. Recognizing these points will also allow us to enjoy the process of getting there. Why hurry?

Finally, there are many of you who would like to take on the role of The Psychic. It's an attractive role, i'll admit, but not

everyone has chosen it as part of their original plan. For
those who didn't select it, the role is a little more
challenging to master. The best roles for you are always
the ones from your original program. The other roles might
be fun to imitate, but they won't help your plan all that
much. At best, those roles might entertain your friends. At
their worst, they will only do harm to the others. Is it worth
the risk?

Chapter 34

The Moralist

i am Nazahah. It wasn't supposed to be like this. *Reality*
was supposed to be wonderfully enjoyable. No one was
supposed to get hurt, or lost. It was a simple idea that
turned horribly complex. Perhaps the guests were given
too much freedom. But, how else could *Reality* have
gathered your interest for such an experience? Already
knowing the deep connection between freedom and
happiness, you wouldn't have agreed to it, in any other
way. Too many restrictions would have driven you from the
opportunity.

Early curiosity within *Reality* combined with this freedom,
allowed you to make many choices that involved trading
acting favors with the others in your world. Many of these
were never repaid during the current lifetime, so you had to
keep returning in order to honor your debts. You simply

ran out of time. As an example of this, let's say one of your friends wanted the experience of royalty, and even though it wasn't supposed to be part of their program, you helped them to experience it. You played the role of servant or advisor for them, and now they owed you and the others some future help with the experiences for which you were searching. Because the roles weren't part of the original plan, they also weren't played very well and it left all of you wanting for something more convincing.

Things got very messy.

That was just a small example, of what I'm trying to describe. As a final point i would add that, at their worst, things had gone beyond anything *Reality* could have imagined. There were some very dark times in your Earth history, where it was thought that there could *never* be a returning from *Reality*, for *any* of you. But it was the gift of freedom, once again, that made all the difference. This time the difference was experienced in another way. Guests started to say *no*.

no to the violence;
no to the cruelty;
no to famine;
no to poverty;
no to slavery;
no to choosing beyond the program.

All of these experiences *had* to be avoided. They just weren't 'fun' anymore. Somehow, we had to restore *Reality's* original purpose.

People started making rules and laws to help guide themselves while in *Reality*, and this definitely helped to improve the experience for everyone. Lifetimes became more enjoyable, again. As hoped, human lifetimes began to grow in length of years *and* in the depth of experience. By limiting the number of experiences to those of their program, people were able to appreciate them more. Sounds simple, doesn't it? Still, even though not *everyone* chooses to use their freedom in this way, it's enough to bring hope to the possibility of your eventual arrival *Home*.

The moralist chooses to do what is correct. They choose to behave in ways that support their lifetime and the lifetimes of others. By staying with the program, they inspire others to do the same. Everyone wins.

Chapter 35

The Prisoner
i am Anak. The moralists and their kind, have seen fit to take my freedom from me. But, it is not my real freedom, only the freedom of movement within the larger field of *Reality*. My limits are only temporary. Soon, I'll have my greater freedom returned to me. But, what choices should i make?

It doesn't matter what i did, or what they thought i did. Here i am. i still have choices; i can still enjoy *Reality* to some extent. i can even complete parts of my program, when the opportunities present themselves. i won't lose hope, and i won't be drawn into drifting from the possibility of my release.

Imprisonment can take on many forms. Do you feel trapped by a situation? Do you recognize any limits upon your experience within *Reality*? Then, we are similar in this. There are bars and restraints of many kinds in our world, and many of them are seen as acceptable, for one reason or another. We even choose to wear them at times, in order to attain some goal of happiness or personal pleasure. We form friendships and financial relationships against our better interests. We seek allies in the struggle, who turn to others when opportunities more favorable steal them away from us. We even feel a sense of injustice around our physical illnesses and challenges. What can we do in these situations? i've already given you part of the answer in my second paragraph.

Choice and timing are relevant to improving conditions for you. If you feel that you can choose to remove yourself from an obligation or a situation, find a moment that is sure to lead to the return of your freedom. Do so honorably, cooperating with the others, fulfilling your original obligations, while avoiding new debts of any kind to the others. There are many who can help you with this, and who won't expect anything in return. Don't look for a temporary return of your freedom, but a more permanent one. Think about long-term goals, and even of possibilities within future lifetimes. *Reality* knows that we can't always get things done, in this one.

Chapter 36

The Scientist

i am Ayah. i'm one of those who wants to be able to prove something, and i'm fascinated with how *Reality* works. i struggle with the possibility that a lot of what i'm experiencing isn't actually real. i enjoy the challenges involved in my search for answers. Perhaps these are what guide my purpose. i'm interested in *knowing*, and this demands evidence. The evidence isn't just for me; it's for everyone! We all feel a sense that things aren't quite *right* with the way the world works, and we want to be able to feel a sense of control over what happens to us, while we're here.

We remember that things are related and connected, even though they seem separate. We know that patterns hide behind everything, and we search to find them. We're naturally curious, and *Reality* gives us plenty with which to work. Some of these mysteries can and *will* be solved during our time here, but not all. They remain for others.

We leave the unfinished work
to the ones who will follow us.

Just when we feel we're close to solving something, a new challenge presents itself. For us, the enjoyment is in the process of discovery. Of course achieving a specific goal is fun, too! But, that happy moment fades quickly, and we're off to solve the next puzzle.

My nature is also creative. i want to bring something new to the world, whether it's a new solution to an old problem, or an original machine for living this lifetime in more, enjoyable ways. More recently, my design efforts have been focused on ways of getting us all *Home*. *Reality* doesn't know this. As long as i'm enjoying my work, *Reality* doesn't tend to get in the way. i feel very close to a solution.

We mostly work with the effects of what's happening. Because of time, we aren't able to reach the *cause*. We know the *cause* happens first; all things originate from the *cause*. But, by the time we measure or see what's happening, the *cause* is gone. It's faster than time, faster than us, and faster than our machines. The only thing we know for certain, is that the *cause was* here. How could it not be? This realization has taught me that we are, essentially, living in the past. Even if it's a delay of less than a second, the present moment has always 'already happened' for us. It exists as an echo. Many of us hope to one-day find the *cause* and to experience the present moment, but these may not be for us to solve. i've, personally, moved on to other ideas. After all, how can someone discover the truth, in what is naturally false?

Chapter 37

The Slave

i am Ebed. We all release some of our self-control and self-knowledge in coming to *Reality*, but i've released more than i should. There's an enjoyable feeling for me in letting someone, or something else have control. At first, it didn't feel like giving up control, because it was a choice i made. But, later, when i tried to take that control back, it didn't feel like it belonged to me anymore. i really like the illusion of *Reality*; i like *everything* about it. It's more than i could *ever* have wanted in an experience. Now, after having been here awhile, i feel as if i want *more* of it. *Reality* likes to give us the things we want.

There's a way to add more illusion to *Reality*, and it's a very clever one. It starts out with little decisions, ones that don't bother us much. We don't start out with the idea of giving up all that control, but with each little movement, within a certain pattern of choices, we cross an invisible limit. Beyond that, the returning becomes much more difficult than first arriving. We all have our programs, and *Reality* wouldn't be unhappy if we were to complete that program, being satisfied with our visit. But it secretly wants us to stay. It wants us to stay *forever*. Without us, *Reality* wouldn't be the same, it might not even exist.

One, small example is in thinking that i have more time than i actually do. i think i'll have time to catch up later in this lifetime, so i stall and avoid playing my parts when the cues are given. i follow in the drama of other characters and start to think that *their* roles are *my* roles, thinking i'm acting, when really I'm not. i sometimes have friends who believe in the same things i do, so it seems perfectly okay to act this way for a while. Deep down though, i know i'm not really lost. And, the idea of avoiding the truth loses its appeal. In the end, knowing this saves me.

We all experience these desires for *more*. Being here is intoxicating, in so many ways. It's so different from where we've come. Thankfully, *Reality* doesn't understand the concept of forever; it only knows limitation. Because of this, it can't keep us here. No matter how hard it tries, we'll always remember who we are, and we'll always find the way *Home*.

Chapter 38

The Believer
i am Aman. i have a sense for the unseen and the unheard within *Reality*. For me these things are as real and alive as anything else. i don't feel the need to prove they exist because personal proof is enough. It sometimes results in long and challenging discussions with the others, but i feel this is only a natural part of our returning *Home*. We struggle to find answers that will guide us and gather us together. i believe the struggle has value.

There are many varieties of faith in our world, each one tailored to individual programs. If these are practiced with devotion and in the spirit of the teachings, each of them can be very fulfilling. These faiths have taken years to develop and have withstood the tests of time, culture and significant political and technological change. Do you belong to one of these? What is your level of commitment? Modern civilization has gradually moved away from an emphasis upon faith in our daily lives, so much so, that many programs now come without their inclusion. A person could live their entire lifetime without this aspect of human experience to enjoy. i wonder at the happiness of such a lifetime. Where do they find a sense of deeper meaning? True, there is meaning to be found in work, family, social and political causes. But, eventually these fade from our lives. What about something more permanent?

Prayer is a 'common thread' that binds our many faiths. It's a great place to begin, and it helps to support us through everything our lifetime offers. There are difficult times, and times of celebration. Each of them can be better experienced in a prayerful attitude. Simply stated, this attitude is one that focuses our attention on what we're doing and saying right *now*. We can turn away from all of the distractions, to focus on this *one* person, this simple act. Are you surprised by this definition? You've had many moments of focus, where the time seemed to slip away, and the concerns of the world were so distant. We've all had them. These moments are prayerful.

There are special experiences that happen to people. i call them *strong moments*, because they produce very strong feelings, thoughts and memories. These experiences can surprise us in a way that is hard to describe. Words aren't enough, to explain what happened to us. *Strong moments* leave us with many questions, that science isn't yet able to answer. If one of these should happen to you, the faith traditions may have the answers. At the very least, they can guide you in finding those answers.

In earlier times, there were brave men and women who would try to remind us of the importance of belief and faith. They faced a lot of resistance and hostility. In *your* time, these messengers are still around to encourage and inspire. Those within the entertainment industries place important messages in the mediums of film and song. These ways seem safer for the messengers, as they share them with us in enjoyable ways. Many times, we don't even realize we're getting a message until later. Some of these modern messengers belong to formal faith traditions, while others see their work in a more artful or psychological way. Their work matters.

Some would like to combine the different faith traditions, but they were actually designed to run side-by-side. Just like the tracks of a train, their paths support and guide us forward. A Scientist or Mathematician might tell you that these paths *do* meet. i like this idea, but i don't think it relates to a situation we can find in *Reality*.

Chapter 39

The Healer

i am Rapha. i can help you with the symptoms of human illness. The symptoms are what seem to bother you most. If it weren't for them, you wouldn't even know your body was sick. When uncomfortable or painful symptoms appear, you want to get your body feeling better, so you can continue to enjoy your stay in *Reality*. There are many kinds of illness and disease in your world. Each one needs special treatment.

When sickness happens, *The Body Sensual* is usually able to fix itself. We just have to give it the time and support it needs. You don't need my help in those situations. But, if the illness stays with your body for a longer period of time, or seems to be getting worse, i am here. This is the common approach to caring for your person. You know this already.

As Alyia mentioned, *Reality* likes to 'nudge' you when you're moving way from the goals of your program. Hint of an illness can be one of those little 'nudges.' It's a respected trait in modern times, to disregard these hints. We want to be seen in a way that supports the image of a strong character. Without proper care, however, strength quickly fades. True, we have been speaking to the importance of acting in *Reality*, but this isn't the kind of acting you should be doing. You are in control of your body, it will do as you command. But, forcing it to work when it needs rest, is misusing your body. The type of acting required by your programming seldom involves your being ill, as part of the scene. If it does require this, you will be asked to 'fake' the illness.

As far as looking for cures, treatments, and finding ways to keep *The Body Sensual* healthy, there are many options available. If i could offer something new to the list, i would recommend a knowledge and understanding of *the eight*. Feel free to read the previous chapters again.

By the way, you're *not* actually sick.
Your body is.
You are *not* your body.
Your body is limited and susceptible;
you are not.

Chapter 40

We are *The Gathering*. You know who we are, and why we've come to you. But, the time has come for us to soon leave you. This choice has been made in order to grant you time to think about all you've read. We won't actually be leaving you, but the communication will pause for a while. The time will pass quickly, and you will accomplish many things. We will be helping you through this period, in our own quiet way.

The most difficult part of your adjustment has been, and will continue to be, your acceptance of this information. You cannot have both, *Reality and Home.* Eventually, one of these must be your focus.

Either *Life* and *Home* are real, or they're not.

As far as your acting is concerned, we'd like to say that you don't need to worry if you find yourself having little in common with the others. You might feel different or alone some of the time, but there is a reason for this. As we search for wholeness in *Reality*, we begin to accept that personal wholeness can only be achieved when we accept ourselves as complete, in relation to our personal part within humanity. All of you together, create the wholeness that comes closest to your memories of *Home*. If humanity was a jigsaw puzzle, your person would be a single piece of that puzzle. As a piece, you are a complete piece: colorful, connected and important to the whole image of the human race. When you play your part, you fit into the picture and your lifetime feels right and good. When you're out of the picture, the whole puzzle starts to destabilize. Confusion grows.

One of the reasons for telling you that there is no hurry in returning *Home,* relates to the previous paragraphs. Just as accepting that the choice between *Reality* and *Home* is an 'all or nothing' situation, so also is the importance of wholeness to returning. We all leave together - *all* of us. No one gets left behind. This may seem unfair, but it is necessary and *possible.* From our point of view, it has already happened. This will change how you feel about the others, about their importance, as being equal to your own. The details about how this will happen can be stated in this way:

We go in our own time.
We arrive at our destination together.

It doesn't make a lot of sense at first, because our ideas around time and space in *Reality* suggest that it's impossible. *Reality* wants us to think in *its* ways. If you think certain things are impossible, you'll never try them. You'll never think to leave.

We will return to you in this way.
There is more to share.

Communications suspended.

Glossary

Home - your Self, *The Gathering*, *The One*, unity, freedom, truth

Life - being alive and aware, existence

Program - Your plan for this lifetime, not written 'in stone', God's Will for you, your Dharma

The Revealing - a brief remembrance of everything, everyone, all of it; similar to an apocalypse, but less cataclysmic, *Word* can be present

Word - a force, or entity that exists beyond duality. It arrives when a sufficient number of individuals are in agreement for the purpose of the common good. Its presence facilitates the achievement of the group's purposes.

The One - created out of the event of *The Gathering's* unification; greater than the combination of the elements that went into its creation; *The One* witnesses, knowing only truth

The Reference Point - a place from which to begin, with eyes wide open and seeing beyond the illusion of *Reality* - a point when *The Gathering* is no longer need as guide

The Attention Space - the present moment and immediate concern within your thinking. This space appears to be limited

Reality - the lifetime and place that one appears to be experiencing, Maya (the illusion)

The Gathering - a collection of beings, similar in nature to angels or aliens

The Pretender - the master actor

The Eight - eight of many current archetypes within *Reality*, they guide and assist with the acting, presented in Article Three (Carri, Alyia, Nazahah, Anak, Ayah, Ebed, Aman, and Rapha)

The *original* - something or someone of which there is only one.

The *cause* - the origin of things and events; it is elusive

Strong moments - 'peak experiences,' religious or mystical experiences

Recommended reading:
The Holy Bible
The Bhagavad Gita
Quran
The Tibetan Book of the Dead
A Course in Miracles and related titles by Marianne Williamson
The Art of Dreaming by Carlos Castaneda
Journeys Out of the Body by Robert Monroe
Anything by Richard Bach
Anything by Shirley MacLaine
Anything by Paolo Coelho
Anything by Carl Jung

Recommended Listening:
Bruce Springsteen
U2
The Beatles
David Bowie
Alanis Morissette
Led Zeppelin

Recommended Viewing:
The Matrix (1999) Wachowski
Waking Life (2001) Linklater
What Dreams May Come (1998) Ward
Contact (1997) Zemeckis
The X-Files (1993-) Carter
Twin Peaks (1990-1991) Lynch/Frost

Recommended Web sites:
Meditations: thespacewithin.podomatic.com

Recommended Activities:
Meditate

Recommended Podcast:
'On Being' with Krista Tippett

Heartfelt gratitude for recent and enduring encouragement:
Nolan Hurd, the students of St. Michael Catholic School, my facebook and Twitter friends, The North Grenville Public Library, McDonalds McCafe coffee, Apple Computers, Susan Cain and The Quiet Revolution, The Light Institute of Galisteo, The Monroe Institute.

About the Author

Michael lives in Ontario, Canada, with his son. He continues to write, while encouraging his students in the discovery of self and other.

His relevant personal and professional background experiences include:
*   15 years as a teacher of Ethics, Philosophy, Religious education and English;
*   Previously published article 'Near Eternal' in the *Journal of the Theosophical Society – Quest;*
*   Previously published article 'Quantum Ascendency' in *Tone Magazine*;
*   Five years living/working in the Kingdom of Saudi Arabia, with excursions to nearby countries that include India, Thailand, and Egypt;
*   Baccalaureate of Arts in Psychology/Religion and Baccalaureate of Education;
•   Meditation instructor and proponent: thespacewithin.podomatic.com

Contact: enterthewitness@gmail.com

Manufactured by Amazon.ca
Bolton, ON

24561759R00090